Yabba Dabba Doo!

...or Never A Star

The Alan Reed Story

by Alan Reed and Ben Ohmart

Published in the USA by:
BearManor Media
PO Box 71426
Albany, Georgia 31708
www.bearmanormedia.com

ISBN 1-59393-313-4

Printed in the United States of America.
Book design by Brian Pearce.

Table of Contents

FOREWORD...5

ON WITH THE SHOW.................................. 11

A YOUNG ACTOR'S JOURNEY......................... 25

THE VILLAGE LIFE.................................... 39

RADIO... 55

EAST OR WEST.. 81

VAUDEVILLE.. 87

LEGITIMATE BROADWAY THEATER 89

MOTION PICTURES................................... 95

TELEVISION 105

OFF CAMERA OR VOICE OVER..................... 109

YABBA DABBA DOO!................................117

APPENDIX 131

CREDITS 149

INDEX.. 205

Foreword

It is unfortunate that money makes the world go around. Because if a publisher 30 years ago thought that he could make enough money on Alan Reed's autobiography, he would have given Alan the green light to complete what he started. They didn't, so Alan didn't finish his life — on paper. What you see here is the complete incomplete writing of a true voice giant. The boisterous voice of Fred Flintstone and Falstaff Openshaw is an integral part of TV and radio history, and it's about time his *story* found a voice as well.

In the introduction to his unpublished memoirs, Alan Reed wrote: "The Author will go backwards and forwards in time throughout the book as the need dictates itself for the progression of the story." It's unfortunate that he didn't progress far enough, because he quit writing the story at a point where his career was just entering radio, with remaining chapters given to synopses in order to interest would-be publishers at the time. I, as "co-author," include everything, every scrap of Reed-written delight, in the name of completion.

If it weren't for Bill Marx (a way I start a good many sentences in my life), there would be no book. His urging led me to Alan's son, Alan Reed, Jr., who was generous beyond measure in making this project happen. He lent me all of his father's papers and photos. I've tried to supplement what I could with the holes that needed to be filled.

Alan Reed, Jr. states that "in his later years Dad was spending more time writing, putting his thoughts on paper. He was taking a course in creative writing, and I think he felt this autobiography assignment might be more challenging if he were to do it in the form of a novel. Declining health was probably why he didn't finish it."

The only alteration I made to his original "exercise" was changing the narrative from the third person to the first person: "He" became "I." I also put his words in bold to separate his text from mine. All else remains the same.

While Alan's chapters are complete, a HUGE thanks goes to Chuck Schaden for allowing me to reprint his *very* fine radio-oriented interview with Alan in the radio chapter, which complements Alan's own words.

And thanks to Kermyt Anderson, Joe Martelle, Stephen Cox, Michael Leannah, John Furek, J. David Goldin (what a radio index!), Jay Hickerson (for his impressive, ultra-helpful *Ultimate History of Network Radio Programming and Guide to ALL Circulating Shows*), David S. Siegel & Susan Siegel (for their wonderfully fun and informative *Radio and the Jews*, still on sale!), Mayumi Ohmart, for *constant* love and support, my mom, Vickie, for letting me watch plenty of *Flintstones* episodes, Randy Bonneville (for a *wealth* of TV and film credits), and Martin Grams, Jr., the greatest radio chronicler of our age, for lots more radio credits than I could find.

I am honored to help bring Alan Reed's memoir to fruition. His body of work is both amazing and diverse. In fact, had I written this book myself, I might have titled it *Not Just a Man Called Flintstone*.

Ben Ohmart
August 2008

In the text that follows, excerpts from Alan Reed's autobiography are set in **bold type** *and slightly indented.*

CHAPTER 1

On With The Show

It was just before midnight and I was watching an old movie on TV, *The Postman Always Rings Twice*. It had been made back in 1945 and I played a featured role in it. My part came on toward the end of the picture — so I hadn't been seen yet — but my name had appeared after the title. The phone rang and a polite voice said, "Mr. Reed, I hope I didn't awaken you. I just wanted to tell you that you're on TV."

"Who is this?" I queried, trying to recognize the voice. I thought it might be one of my sons trying to fool the old man.

"Oh, you don't know me. I'm just a fan."

"Come on, quit kidding," I replied. "Who is it?"

"I'm not kidding, sir," the polite voice answered. "Last week I saw your picture in the paper in connection with your fifty-sixth anniversary in show business. I've been a fan for at least thirty of those fifty-six years. So I looked you up in the phone book when I saw your name on the TV screen, and I thought I'd call you to let you know that you have a fan."

By this time I believed him and said, "Well, thank you, sir. That's very kind of you," and after a few pleasantries I said good night and hung up.

I was touched. It was a rare happening, because in all of my years in the entertainment industry, I had never been a star, in the true sense of the word. I am what's known as a character actor, and while many of my "characters" have had national prominence, my name is relatively unknown. While many kind people through the years have expressed appreciation of my work, the above-described midnight phone call was a first — and it set me to thinking: Here I was at almost 70, Alan Reed, a still-working character actor. Fifty-six of those years had been spent in (or close to) the entertainment industry.

Fifty-six working years is a long time in a business that is noted for short-lived careers. Fifty-six years! I thought of the gradual changes that had taken place in the different branches of the entertainment industry in which I had participated. I had seen the small-time stock companies almost completely vanish. I had seen vaudeville give way to motion pictures, radio come on like a giant only to be replaced by television which stole from movies and radio and forever changed both. I had witnessed the fall of great stars who could not make the transition from one medium to another.

As I thought back through the years, I remembered my first professional job.

I was fourteen and, through a most unusual theatrical agent, got two weeks as an extra with the visiting French Opera Comique at the old Jolson Theatre in New York. The agent who sent me over for the job was the eighty-three-year-old uncle of one of Broadway's most famous producers — Edgar Selwyn. The Selwyn Building, which housed the huge Selwyn Theatre, ran through from 42nd Street to 43rd Street. Above the theatre was a fourteen-story office building. It was filled with all kinds of tenants — but mostly people in one phase or another of show business. Most were small one- or two-room offices with entrances from the corridors of the building.

Except one.

On the 5th floor was a literal "hole in the wall." It had probably been meant for a closet to house utilities, but entrée to the halls had never been opened and the only way to get to it was through a large window from the fire escape on 43rd Street. So the aspiring young actor had to climb five flights of steep iron stairs and step across the windowsill into a room about ten feet square — just large enough for one desk and a bulletin board — which listed all the theatres in town. After each theatre were numerals: 4 – 18 – 9 – 38, etc.

Edgar Selwyn had wanted to provide useful work for his eighty-three-year-old uncle and had set him up in this unused closet as a no-rent clearing house for extras. The numerals represented the number of "atmosphere" people needed at each theatre. A friend had told me about Selwyn's old uncle who had a monopoly on supplying this need. Each extra got $1 per performance, out of which the agent got 10 cents. In all, I later learned, he booked about 300 extras per week in season at 80 cents per (there were eight performances weekly) for an average of $240 a week for himself — a goodly sum in 1921, especially for an eighty-three-year-old man who had been a pants presser most of his life.

He was a sweet old man, short, slightly stout, bespectacled. There was a twinkle in his eyes, a warmth he unsuccessfully tried to hide behind what he thought was a brusque, businesslike exterior. In season, his little cubbyhole was packed — shoulder to shoulder — with men, women, boys and girls of all ages, waiting to get a blue strip from Mr. Solomon, which meant at least $7.20 for a week's work. If they were lucky and the show proved a hit — it was a career.

But on the hot, humid New York summer day that this young Teddy Bergman (later to become Alan Reed) entered this unusual office, it was empty, except for Mr. Solomon. He was sitting at his desk in his underwear, fanning himself. As I stepped over the windowsill he exclaimed in an unmistakable accent, "Oy gevalt — anudder vun."

"Another what?" I asked.

"Anudder idiot," he replied. "Who else but a stupid schmo vould climb five flights stairs on a day like dis, ven for five cents on de subvay he could be at Cooney Island swimming in de Hotlantic?"

"I want to be an actor," my fourteen-year-old in-between voice replied, trying to sound artistic.

"Den you're a double schmo," said Mr. Sarcasm, as he continued in a sing-song voice, "In de summer — in New York, even ektors who vant to be ektors don't get no voik. De teeyaters are almost all closet and dey don't open till efter Labor Day."

"But," I interrupted, "I can only work during my school vacation."

"In dot case," he sing-songed, "deliver ice, it's cooler."

"Oh well, I tried," this disappointed thespian philosophized. "Thanks anyway," and I started to step over the windowsill.

"Vot are you running?" said Mr. Solomon. "Did I tell you I couldn't get you a job?"

"Well, I thought you did," I naively said.

"Sit down — stop being a schmo," sang Mr. About Face. I looked for a non-existent chair, then sat on the windowsill.

"In de foist place," continued Mr. Underwear, "in my office until I tell you you didn't got a job — you got it."

"But you said…"

"Zell zive shach!" he exploded.

This was my grandparent's language, and I knew it meant "shut up."

"Yes sir," I meekly replied.

Mr. Solomon continued. "You're ah lucky boy — ten minutes before you came in I got a call from de only show dot's opening in de summer heat. I tink dey're mashooge, but de French Opera Comical opens tonight and dey need four extras to carry a king around on a chair vit poles — two on each end. You're ah husky boy — you can do it. Do you spik French?"

"No sir, I…"

"Tsawright, dehy'll teach you. Here's your slip — go to de Jolson Theatre right away and tonight you're an ektor. Good luck, boychick."

Thus it was. I was overjoyed, and as I effusively thanked this warm, kindly old man sitting in his strange cubbyhole in his underwear, I didn't have the heart to tell him that his fly was open. In retrospect, it was *quite* an interview.

Between that first job and today there have been many exciting highlights. One occurred just after my formal education came to an abrupt halt in my second year at Columbia University School of Journalism.

I was playing the leading role in what was then called the Variety Show. On the third night a florid-faced man, wearing a wide-brimmed Western Stetson came backstage and asked for me. In those days in New York City a Western Stetson was a most uncommon sight and all eyes followed its progress to my dressing room. The wearer turned out to sound quite different from what the viewers had expected.

In a voice heavy with overtones of a New York City merchant, he said, "Teddy Bergman? My name is Ralph Rose, and if you're interested in professional acting I've got a proposition for you! Can we go somewhere and have a cup of coffee and I'll tell you about it."

My eyes bugged as my 18-year-old mind saw visions of theatre marquees emblazoning forth

THEODORE BERGMAN
IN
THE MERCHANT OF VENICE

"Yes, sir," I replied. "Be right with you!"

Why *The Merchant of Venice*? Because that's where the bug that infects all actors was born. So, for the moment we'll leave Ralph Rose and his proposition temporarily and go backwards six and a half years in time to my graduating class in Public School 52, New York City.

Miss Frances Malone, my homeroom teacher, was a most progressive and gifted woman who believed in exposing her pupils to many fields of endeavor. There were trips to museums, factories, farms and the theatre. Miss Malone took the class to a matinee to see Fritz Lieber — a leading Shakespearean actor of the day — in *The Merchant of Venice*. The magnificent performance (it might have been hammy but to my unknowledgeable mind it was glorious), the brilliant costumes, the colorful settings and the beautiful light changes all did their share to start that virus growing inside my 11 ½-year-old self.

I emerged from the performance on soaring wings. All the way back to school I rhapsodized to Miss Malone about the wonders that I beheld. Frances Malone was an unusual teacher possessed of a keen insight. I was the youngest student in her class and very bright. (I had skipped grades three times and was being sent to Townsend Harris High School.) Townsend Harris was part of the College of the City of New York for exceptional students. The normal four-year high school course was completed there in three years.

Miss Malone came to a quick decision.

"Teddy," she said, with the bit of lilt in her voice that was what remained of her Irish immigrant grandfather, "how would you like to play Shylock as part of our graduating class program?"

Enthusiasm welled up bubblingly as I shouted, "Wow! Could I? Oh boy! Wait'll I tell my mom!"

My mom wasn't around during the day. After she gave me breakfast and a packed lunch she had to rush to the subway for the hour ride to her job in downtown Manhattan. She made $30 a week. This, with the $12 weekly alimony check she received from my father, was enough to keep us fairly well fed in a three-room apartment in the new community of Inwood, in upper Manhattan.

When we had moved there, the terrifying experiences of hearing my parents fighting was still fresh in my seven-year-old mind. I remembered hiding under the dining room table and crying at the horrible things they were calling each other.

"Cheater! Adulterer!" This shrieking, screaming sound could not be coming from my mother, who was usually so soft spoken.

And, "You bitch! It's your father's fault that I went to another woman!"

Of course, I didn't understand the words, but the sounds were frightening and different from any I had ever heard. And this time my crying didn't stop them. That was the last night the three of us slept under the same roof.

Except for occasional weekends, I didn't see my father for ten years — ten years of hearing my old man vilified by my mother, my uncles and aunts, and the autocratic patriarch of the family — my grandfather.

Abraham Greenberg had come to America from a small village in Russia. He had slipped out to avoid a 25-year mandatory enlistment in the Russian army, leaving his pregnant young wife Esther with the promise to send money for her passage before the baby was due. Nobody in the small "shtetl" believed he could do it — but he did. He was a shrewd, resourceful young man who worked hard at odd jobs and saved every penny he could. He was a glazier, a painter — anything that would produce a buck. Two days after her arrival in New York Esther was delivered of twins — a boy and a girl. The girl, my mother, was the elder by ten minutes.

My grandfather brought with him an old world strictness of behavior with which he and Esther raised their children. Abraham allowed no departure from his didactic way of thinking. An apt description would be "despotic." All except three of my uncles grew to adulthood with the same limited attitude as their father who completely dominated them and their thinking. This included my mother and the grandchildren as they came along. My first thirteen years came under this influence.

Abraham and Esther also brought from the old country an indisputable belief in Orthodox Judaism. I often wondered in later years how this supposed piety allowed for the aggressive "no holds barred" business sense that provided Abraham with three fortunes in his long lifetime. My mother Rachael was raised in luxury. By the time she married Henry Bergman, Abraham and a partner owned four solid blocks of tenements in the Yorkville section of New York City. He also held a contract from the city to paint and decorate all of the schools in the five boroughs. This was in 1906.

Abraham had learned the political game. At the outset, he had objected to the marriage mainly because he and his family were "Litvaks" while Henry Bergman's family were "Galitzianers." This merely meant that they had come over from Austria. There were small differences in the pronunciation of Yiddish, each being influenced by the mother country. Each group thought itself superior to the other and each held the other in contempt. There was another reason for the objection. At that time Abraham's fortune (including the Yorkville holdings) was considerable — about $10,000,000 on paper — while Henry Bergman was just two years out of New York University's Law School and had only recently started in practice.

However, for once, Abraham allowed his oldest daughter to follow her heart. With all of the background of wealth, Rachel remained a rather simple, honest, religious woman who became infatuated with the handsome, urbane young lawyer. After a lavish wedding and a short honeymoon they settled down in an apartment in New York's then fashionable Washington Heights area. Unfortunately it was only one block from Abraham and Esther's five-story private brownstone residence. This was a mistake. Abraham's domination continued.

The year 1907 brought two events of importance to the two families. That was the year of a great financial panic and Abraham and his partner lost all of their heavily mortgaged Yorkville holdings. This reduced Abraham's fortune to about one-tenth of its original size and turned him into a tight-fisted and very embittered man. It was also the year that I was born, on August 20th.

The marriage of Henry and Rae Bergman lasted eight years — seven of them relatively tranquil. In the interim Mom and I spent as much time in the big brownstone townhouse as in our own apartment. I was adored by my aunts and uncles and grandparents. In the summer there were trips to the farm my grandfather owned in Sullivan County. There was a fine "swimmin' hole" and I could climb trees and roll down the steep grass-covered hill in back of the farmhouse. My dad would come up weekends and I always looked forward to the romps we would enjoy and the walks through the woods. But when the weekends were over, the family would again refer to my father as the "Galitzianer." I didn't understand, but there was something disturbing about the tone of his voice.

Henry's law practice grew little by little. He now had two clerks and worked long hours himself, but, of course, couldn't begin to take care of his wife in the manner in which she had been brought up. Rae didn't complain — she tried her best to make do. However, her wardrobe was wearing out and she badly needed a warm coat for the cold New York winter.

This brought on the tragedy that culminated in the divorce.

My father had seen the need and acted on it: He bought her a fur coat. To do this he used funds that he shouldn't have. He had collected a $3500 judgment for a client who was in Europe. The client had told him that he would not be back for six months. Henry had more than enough in fees that would be due him before that client's expected return. So he "borrowed" $2000 from the collected fund and bought the fur coat. Then the roof fell in!

The client returned within two weeks because of the impending war in Europe, and demanded the money due him. Henry gave him the remaining $1500 and told him he'd have the balance in a day or two. The client left, a very angry man. Henry tried frantically to raise the money, but he couldn't. He was desperate. He had nowhere to go but to Rae and her father. Red-faced, he confessed the whole episode to his wife. Rae's first reaction was: "Oh, my God — how could you! You stole money!"

"I did it for you, darling. You needed the coat and I wanted to show that father of yours that I could at least keep my wife warm and looking decent."

"Oh, Henry!" she sobbed. "We'll take the coat back first thing in the morning!"

Which they did — but the merchant pointed out that it was now used merchandise and he could only give them $1,000 for it. They said they'd think about it and departed, knowing there was only one course left.

"Rae," mumbled Henry. "We must go to your father. I'd rather cut my throat, but the hell with pride. This is no time for it."

"You're right. Poppa will understand."

"I hope so. He hates my guts, but I don't think he can be that inhuman. I'll show him my books and when he sees that shortly I'll have more than enough to pay him back, he'll have to lend me the money."

So my parents went to the fateful meeting with Abraham. Henry told the whole story, showed his books, and ended desperately by saying, "I'll give you my note!"

"Take your goddamn note and stick it!" shouted Abe. "You're a crook and a no-good and I vouldn't give you a penny if you were starving from hunger. I told my Rachele all along she never should of married you — and now it comes out! You're a dirty, rotten thieving galitzianer and I vant you outa my family. Out! Out! You somafabich. You got yourself into this, get yourself out of it. Now get de hell outta here!"

They left. Henry was furious and sick; Rachel, as always, was completely cowed by her father.

The client came back for his money, refused the thousand dollars that Henry told him he could raise on the coat, and brought charges against him to the Bar Association. Result — Henry was disbarred! He could no longer practice law.

He got a job selling cigars at $30 a week. Rae tried her meager best to keep things going at home, but she was no match for the combined onslaught of her single-minded family. They urged getting rid of Henry and coming home to live with little me who had just started school. This turmoil took the heart out of Henry. He found little peace at home and turned elsewhere for solace — and sex. Sensing this, Rae followed him like a detective, made a big scene when she caught Henry and his inamorata lunching together, which led up to the frightening shouts I heard, terrified, under the dining room table.

Of course, I didn't get my father's side of the sordid episode until I was seventeen. Henry had married again, this time to a highly intelligent woman who had been secretary to Governor Lehman of New York. They had a daughter. My half-sister, Jeanne, was about fifteen years my junior. During those interim years Henry had found his true forte: sales. He had gone to work for a relatively small credit checking agency. In a very short time he became sales manager and, through his efforts alone, had tripled the amount of business. He felt that his efforts warranted a partnership and he asked for it.

"Jim, I've been with you for six years now, and you must admit I've done a helluva job for you."

"No doubt about it, Henry, and I think the bonuses you received have shown our appreciation."

"They have, Jim, they have — but not enough. The way I see it, I personally have brought in more than twice the number of accounts you had when I started. Now I think that warrants a full partnership."

"Whoa — wait a minute," oiled Jim. "This company is now worth a lot of money. Do you have enough to buy a half interest?"

Henry was furious. "Buy? *Buy*? Why, you ignorant bastard!" he shouted. "You can't see the future — only the immediate buck. Can't you understand that with me as a partner we can grow and grow until we dominate the field? I wouldn't be surprised if one day we might even put Credit Clearing House out of business."

Credit Clearing House was then second only to Dun & Bradstreet in the credit checking industry. They were first in the garment trades, millinery and furs — the fields in which Henry had been working.

"Don't make me laugh!" snapped Jim. "You're a dreamer. Credit Clearing House — hah! Lemme tell you something, Henry. In this business a dollar is a dollar and if you can't put up — that's it."

Henry became deadly calm. "Okay, mastermind, if that's the way you want it. Okay. So you think I'm a dreamer. Well, I'll tell you a little dream I'm going to make come true. I'm starting my own business and we'll soon see how long you can hold on to all the accounts I've brought in. Goodbye, Jim. You've made a bad mistake."

So, in a one-room office Henry Bergman started The Credit Exchange. In less than three years Jim was out of business and The Credit Exchange moved to much larger quarters occupying a whole floor in a large office building at 38th Street and Broadway. Eventually it became a national organization with offices in Philadelphia, Chicago and Los Angeles, and its home office occupied two huge floors of a block-long building at 34th Street and Eighth Avenue. This expansion needed much capital and Henry had to take in investment partners so that his holdings were reduced to 25%.

I was inordinately proud of my father as I watched his business grow through the succeeding years. A camaraderie grew between us as we met as adults which meant more than the meager father-son relationship that had existed during my school days while my father was building a life around a new marriage. Between my 8th and 11th years I saw my father only intermittently — and on those occasions only at his office. He had felt — though he did not explain it at the time — that his daughter Jeanne was far too young to accept or understand a previous marriage and the fact that she had a brother.

At my grandfather's insistence I worked at a variety of jobs during my summer vacations from school. It was mostly during these times that I would meet my father for lunches and from year to year I could watch the growth of his business. I worked as an office boy, a stock clerk, a relief elevator operator, a telephone switchboard operator and as an assistant shipping clerk for a cotton goods converter. Of course I didn't realize it at the time but all of these jobs were giving me an opportunity to meet and work with a variety of people — a definite plus for an actor-to-be. The bug was still biting away inside of me.

"An ektor! An ektor you vanna be! A bum — dot's vot a ektor is," shouted my almost incoherent grandfather. "You'll be a business man. Dot's all — no argument! I forbid it!"

"But, Grandpa — "

"No buts. An ektor! An ektor couldn't support his mother!"

This was before I left my grandfather's religion and, in effect, shook off the old man's hold on me. It happened in the synagogue during the High Holidays. There is a portion of the services concerning the High Priests. (Anybody whose name is Cohen automatically becomes a High Priest. They're supposed to be descended from the "Cohanim" of Biblical times.) At a point the High Priests, covered with ancient prayer shawls, chant a three- or four-thousand-year-old melody. It is supposed to be an awesome moment.

I, seated next to Abraham, heard my grandfather whisper to me, "You not allowed to look on dem — it's too holy — if you do vunce you'll go blind, and if you look twice, you'll drop dead."

"Baloney," I thought. "These are just a bunch of guys named Cohen." So I looked twice and nothing happened and out the window went the whole religion.

It wasn't until many years later that a learned cousin of mine told me that my grandfather had just been questioning my quickness of wit. It was a conundrum — the answer — if you went blind the first time you looked, how *could* you look a second time? I was aghast at my childish lack of perception when I heard this. But by then it was too late. I had formed my own form of religion. While I most certainly believed in a Supreme Being or Force, I felt that all of the rituals and adornments of the organized religion were nothing more than a diversion to entice and hold mankind within each particular sect.

I felt that the essence of all religions was to be found in the Ten Commandments, The Sermon on the Mount and an honest application of the Golden Rule. One of my early writings, a free verse poem, concerned itself with my religious thoughts.

Unspoken Prayer
by Theodore Bergman

Time and again in the deep of night
Or the busy turmoil of the working day
My heart had said a prayer...
Asked silently for YOUR bounty
Asked for what it knew existed...
YOUR understanding.

For YOUR ear is everywhere
YOUR eye ubiquitous
YOU and YOU alone
Can sense all creation.
For even the thought that skims so lightly
In my brain
And the unuttered stirring in my heart
Are of YOUR inspiration.

What need then for the vocal chantings
Of the many...in the special house?
Why the ritual and the oft-repeated words?

When it is only the true intent of the heart
That YOU seek out.

But going back to that High Holiday in the synagogue: it was not only the last time I accompanied my grandfather, but although I didn't realize it at the time, it was the moment I shook off his hold on me and decided to go my own way.

CHAPTER 2

A Young Actor's Journey

I sat in the coffee shop listening to Ralph Rose, the man in the western hat.

"I run this stock company in Oklahoma City," he was saying. "Frankly, it's a hobby of mine. I didn't make it as an actor so I went into the candy business. Now I own a pretty good wholesale candy factory. It makes me enough to have fun with my theatre. We do a different show each week, and I'd like to hire you to do general business. I think you've got the makings."

"What's general business?" I asked.

Mr. Rose smiled. "In a stock company the permanent company is made up of a leading man and woman, a male and female character actor and — general business — which means you'll get to play a wide variety of roles. You'd be our juvenile, our second character man, you'd play kids and sometimes even a female — whatever comes along. For walk-ons and bits we use local people."

"Sounds good," I said, trying to be cool. "How much does it pay?"

"Oh, right down to business, eh? Well, why not? I pay $50 a week and you can sleep at my house. That's just my son and myself. He's twelve and a violin prodigy. Well? How does it sound to you?"

Ralph Rose was a warm, pleasant man and I liked him and his direct approach right off. But this had happened so quickly.

"Mr. Rose, I —"

"Ralph," beamed the entrepreneur.

"Ralph, I can't give you an answer now. It's a big step. It's also a good opportunity, as you describe it. I'll certainly have to talk it over with my mother, and I'll have to decide if I want to quit my education."

But, deep inside, I had already decided.

"Take your time, my boy. I didn't really expect an answer right away. I'll be in New York for a while and I'll hold the job open for you until the middle of next week. You can reach me here."

He gave me his business card on which he had penciled a New York telephone number.

"Okay, Mr. — er, Ralph, I'll call you as soon as I can."

Mr. Rose paid the check and we parted. I walked to the subway stepping on air. At home I found my mother waiting up for me.

"Why so late?" she asked.

"Oh, Mom, wait'll you hear!" And I excitedly poured out the evening's events.

"But your education — We've both worked hard so that you could finish school and get your degree. That's been my dream — my son, a college graduate. You could become a very good writer. No, I can't let you run off to the middle of nowhere because you think you want to be an actor!"

"I don't *think*, Mom. I *know*! I've really been wasting my time studying journalism. My heart isn't in it. This can be an opportunity to start learning to do what I've wanted to do ever since I played Shylock as a kid. You don't know — you can't know — what happens to me when I get on a stage before an audience. My whole body acts up. I — I tingle. Every time I'd do a play at school or at the temple I became a different person. I was so happy, I could bust. And that week and a half when I worked in cousin Harry's act at the Palace and the Riverside I didn't ever want it to *end*. (Cousin Harry was Harry Green, a vaudeville star of the first magnitude. More about this episode — my introduction to vaudeville — later.) You don't know, Mom, what a tough time I had going back to school after that. I was miserable. So, please, Mom, *please, please* tell me I can *go*!"

"Oh, Teddy, Teddy — it's too serious a decision. We'll have to talk to Grandpa."

"We will like hell! If you think I'm gonna let that old phony tell me what to do with my life, you've got another think coming! Mom, I want you to know I appreciate how hard you've worked and sacrificed to get me through school, and until I could help a little by my summer jobs, to support me, but I can't let even you decide what I'm gonna do with my life! I'm gonna think about it a little more, but the chances are I'm going to Oklahoma City!"

Next day I called my father and gave him all the details. We had long since discussed my innermost feelings about becoming an actor.

A young Alan Reed.

"Son," he said, "you've got to follow your heart. If a man is happy in the work he is doing, he has a much better chance for success. I say go — and good luck."

Oklahoma City was a surprise to me. I knew it was the largest city in the state, yet to a born and bred New Yorker it was a hick town. New Yorkers had, and probably still have, an over-exaggerated opinion of themselves in relation to the rest of the country. I had never been beyond New York State and was not prepared for the simplified openhandedness that greeted me as Ralph introduced me to the taxi driver who was to drive us out to Ralph's home.

"Right glad to meeche, neighbor. Jes you set in the back an ah'll take yo luggage up front with me."

"Er — thank you — neighbor," said I who was good at picking up dialects. "Ah'll jus do that."

Ralph chuckled to himself. "Pretty good, boy, pretty good. You're gonna find things and people a lot different out here. The pace is slower and the people are a lot kinder. I think you'll like it after awhile."

"Yep. Ah reckon you're right, podner," I mimicked.

The drive to Ralph's house was beautiful. We went through a lot of open country, past some beautiful homes and an occasional oil derrick. Ralph's place was smaller than the more pretentious homes we'd passed, but it was very inviting, sort of a ranch house, very trim, white with contrasting shutters in dark green. As we drove up beautiful violin music was emanating from the house.

"That's Junior," said Ralph proudly.

"Wow!" I wowed. "I had no idea he was that good!"

Ralph smiled happily and mimicked Al Jolson: "You ain't heard nothin' yet!"

"Ah'll take the bags in, Mr. Rose." The taxi driver was a tall, thin fellow who folded out of his car with difficulty.

"Thank you, Slim," Ralph said, and in an aside to me, "You can't find 'em like that in New York."

As we entered the house the music stopped and a slight twelve-year-old replica of his father entered the hallway and waited shyly to be introduced.

"Junior, this is the young man I wrote you about — Teddy Bergman. He's going to live with us."

"Howdy. I'm pleased to meet you." Junior stuck out his hand.

"Hi." I shook the kid's mitt. "I heard you practicing as we drove up. You sure can play that fiddle."

"Oh. I was just noodling around," responded Ralph Rose, Jr.

"Well, you go noodle some more," said his old man, "while I show Teddy to his room. Here's your money, Slim, and thanks for helping. See you at the theatre."

"Yes, sir," said Slim, pocketing his fare. "Right nice to meet ya, Mr. Bergman. Well, ah'll be skedadlin'. See ya at the theatre."

The brass bed in my good-sized bedroom looked particularly inviting to me after the long journey and lack of proper sleep on the train. I stretched out on it and asked Ralph, "What did Slim mean when he said 'see you at the theatre?' Is he coming to the first show?"

Ralph laughed. "No. He works for me part time. He helps build scenery and string lights and sometimes even does a walk-on or a bit. His cab is on special call but mostly he just picks up people at the station. Slim's a very handy guy. Now, why don't you take a nap and I'll go do the same, and I'll have Junior get us up in time for supper — or do you call it dinner?"

My eyes were already closed as I mumbled incoherently, "I call it … zzzz."

Ralph tiptoed out of the room.

He had come to like this husky young actor. He sensed a real dedication and he admired the way I had made my decision. On the train trip out I had told of the scene with my mother, of my disavowal of my grandfather's hold on me and of the conversation with my father. It took a lot of guts. This boy would go far, he thought. He had watched me act and saw a natural talent. In the college play I played Hendrik Hudson and the Dutch accent I used had seemed so real that he was surprised to hear me talk straight English tinged with a bit of New Yorkese. He'd heard me clown a bit with the dining room steward and then with Slim, and Ralph now realized that I was a natural dialectician and mimic. We had shared a compartment on the train and Ralph had been impressed by my spectacular muscular development. I modestly told him that I'd won a heavyweight division title in wrestling under Coach Gus Petersen at Columbia. All this drifted through my mind as I lay down for my nap.

At dinner that evening I learned much more about my host and his family. Mrs. Rose lived in another part of town; she and Ralph had been divorced about two years before. It had been an amicable divorce. Both felt they'd be happier living apart. On occasion they would get together and Mrs. Rose ran the box office at the theatre. Mrs. Thompson, a not too far away neighbor, came in to clean and cook — which she had done tonight. The beef stew was delicious. When the meal was over and Junior had gone to study, Ralph confided his future plans for the kid.

"Leopold Auer! The greatest!"

"The greatest what?" I wanted to know.

"The greatest teacher of violin in America — perhaps in the whole world. He now lives in New York and I got an appointment with him last week. When I told him about Junior's accomplishments he said he'd listen to the kid if I brought him to New York.

But he was frank. He told me that nine times out of ten talks like this turn out to be parent's misguided pride rather than the discovery of a genius talent."

"Look, Ralph. I don't know a thing about classical music, but are you sure Junior does have a real talent?"

"Teddy, I don't know all that much about music myself. But my judgment is not based on what *I* know. The finest musical experts in the state have proclaimed the kid a genius. He's been studying since he was four years old. He's progressed from one teacher to another until for the past two years he's been working with the top maestro in this area. His teacher is the conductor of the Oklahoma State Philharmonic. Junior has made three solo appearances with that orchestra, and each one was a resounding success. He's hailed throughout the region as a most unusual prodigy. If he is taught by Auer he can become one of the world's leading concert artists! Whew! When I get wound up on the kid's possibilities I don't know when to stop. Ha, ha — who the hell is Misha Elman?"

I was truly impressed. Ralph's fountain of words had made a believer of me. It also taught me something that was to contribute to the merchandising of my own talents in later years… "If you're gonna sell anything — yourself included — you've gotta *believe* in the product."

Ralph suggested that we get a good night's sleep because tomorrow was to be a long and busy day. I didn't need any coaxing.

The next morning we went first to the candy factory. It was a four-story building on the outskirts of the city. I was intrigued with the machinery — and the candy. Ralph was busy inspecting each department as he looked over the piled up mail, signed checks, dictated a few letters to his efficient secretary, and made phone calls. It was noon before we left for the theatre.

My first reaction to the exterior of the building was disappointment. No glamorous marquee, no electric displays, just a painted sign above the plain doorway that proclaimed: "The Ralph Rose Stock Company." On either side of the door was a metal frame about 18"x24." Inside of one was the name of the first play and its author, and prominently printed on the cardboard insert: "Directed by Ralph Rose." The other frame listed the permanent members of the company, my name included. Also on the right of the doorway was a rather small box office window. I had known from my reading of the theatrical trade papers of the great stock companies then running — The Stuart Walker Co. in Cincinnati, The Jessie Bonstelle Detroit Civic Theatre and, of course, the famous Eilitch's Gardens of Denver. I had seen pictures of magnificent edifices which housed these companies so by comparison, my first reaction was a distinct let down.

In reality, the Ralph Rose Company was no better or no worse than hundreds of other companies throughout the country. It was probably classified as third rate, but it brought theatre to its local area, and its customers were satisfied. Some came regularly, others occasionally, with the result that the theatre had to be subsidized from the profits of the candy company.

The interior of the theatre was better than the outside. The walls were of a rich looking brocade, the seats a dark red mohair, and the stage and lighting equipment seemed good to my inexperienced eyes. There were four small dressing rooms, one each for the leading man and the leading lady, and one each for the other men and women.

At 2 p.m., after Ralph had shown me through the theatre, and we'd had a bite of lunch at the drug store on the corner, I met my fellow players and the reading of the first play of the season began. In it I found I had to double — play two parts. I was an old farmer and a seemingly retarded young carpenter. It turned out he wasn't retarded at all — he was just shy — especially where the ingénue was concerned. By the last act I had patented an invention and married the girl. It was a good opportunity and got me off to a fine start as the new member of the company.

The first week in a stock company is always the easiest for the actors — they have only one play to learn. But from then on — murder! The minute the first play opens the cast starts learning and rehearsing the next one. Inasmuch as the plays were only of one week's duration, it was rehearse all day, play at night, then study lines for the next day's rehearsal.

Ralph was a mediocre director, but he kept things moving. He was of the old melodramatic school while I was trying for the natural approach then coming into vogue. The rest of the cast was just adequate. The character people were definitely of the old school, and the leading man and woman somewhere in between. But it was a beginning for me and a learning period. I was able to save a good part of my salary after sending money to my mother each week. As the months went by I had the feeling that I might have to unlearn many of the acting ways I had picked up. I also noticed a change in Ralph who seemed to be getting more and more depressed.

"What's the matter, Ralph?" I asked during a lunch break. "You're not your old happy self anymore."

"I got troubles, Teddy. Big troubles. It's the candy business. Two of my largest accounts have gone bankrupt. I'll be lucky if I get five cents on the dollar. And, as you've probably noticed, the box office receipts have fallen off. Frankly, I'm worried about survival."

"What a lousy break," I sympathized. "But you'll pull through. Keep your chin up."

But Ralph didn't pull through. His creditors demanded payment, the banks refused any additional loans, the attendance at the theatre fell off considerably, and finally, in my thirty-eighth week of employment, Ralph just managed to save himself from bankruptcy by using his life's saving and selling his home to pay off all debts. All except a few of the theatre company; personnel refused Ralph's offer to pay them to the end of their contracts. They had enjoyed the good years with Ralph and now were willing to help in this trying situation. I too was grateful for the opportunity that Ralph had given me. I had managed to save close to $800 and was, in truth, anxious to get back to New York. I had made up my mind to enroll in the American Academy of Dramatic Arts as I didn't think this meager theater experience was sufficient to serve as the foundation for a career.

Ralph too had decided to go to New York with Junior for the long-anticipated interview with Leopold Auer. This time the travel was different. The two Roses shared a lower berth and I took the upper. During the journey Ralph confided to me: "Boy, I'm in a helluva spot. All I've managed to salvage out of that whole mess is about $900. I'd hoped to have enough to open a small homemade candy shop, but I didn't make it. It would take about $2,000 at least. I guess I'll have to look for a job as a candy maker."

I had a crazy idea. I'd always had a bit of a gambling streak in me and I'd been in some crap games with both good and bad luck. Now I said to Ralph: "Look, I know where there's a big crap game — It's in the basement of a hotel in Long Beach, Long Island. It takes a minimum stake of $500 to get into it. Suppose I put up $250 and you do the same. Maybe I can get lucky and hit a few passes and we might win enough for you to open a store."

"No, Teddy," said the worried Ralph. "I've got to nurse the few dollars that I have as far as I can. I don't know how long it'll take me to get a job. The kid and I have to live while I'm looking, and I'm hoping Mr. Auer will agree to teach Junior after he hears him play. I'll have to pay him — at least a down payment until I get going."

"Listen, Ralph," I persisted with the enthusiasm of youth. "You might as well be broke as the way you are. Going into business is a gamble at the start anyway. Take a chance. If we lose, I'll still have a few hundred left of my savings and I'll lend you that if you need it. And besides, there's something I didn't tell you: My mother has just moved into a larger apartment at 99th Street and Broadway with her youngest brother, the only one of her family who got to college. He's now a dentist and is about to start a practice in the front two rooms of the apartment. It's a railroad type of place. It has nine rooms altogether. My mom and I will only use the kitchen and two bedrooms. She plans to rent out the other four rooms for extra income. If worse comes to worse, you'll at least have a roof over your heads 'til you get started. After what you did for me, taking me into your house and all, she'll be only too happy for the opportunity of paying you back. Well, what do you say? Give it a go?"

"Man, you are one helluva salesman!" said the astonished Ralph. "Alright, we'll give it a go."

Ralph's decision served to remove the aura of gloom that had surrounded the trip up to that point. Even Junior's spirits seemed to lift. The balance of the journey to New York was spent in an atmosphere of gaiety as Ralph and I recounted some of the closing-night antics for Junior.

Free of the discipline of the larger theatres, the cast was allowed the privilege of playing tricks on each other on closing nights. This served as a release from the arduous day and night regimen that they had followed during the week. The Saturday performance had the largest attendance and the audiences looked forward to the unusual. They never knew what to expect. At any moment a different, rib-tickling line of dialog might pop up — or a piece of business meant to "break up" the other members of the cast. Many of the regulars came on closing nights of a play even though they'd seen it earlier in the week. These antics became prime topics of conversation throughout the following days.

I told Junior, "Your pop had warned me about these tricks but I was so busy learning lines and playing at night, I'd forgotten about them. Well, in the third act I'm sittin' on the couch with Marcia, the ingénue. We're playing a very tender, soft love scene when all of a sudden from behind the couch we hear 'Hearts and Flowers' being hummed — not too softly — by Barry and Rosemary, our leading man and lady."

"What did you do?" asked Junior.

"Well, Marcia and I looked at each other. Marcia winked with her upstage eye and we tried to play the rest of the scene. But the humming went on a little louder and by then the audience was laughing like mad, my voice got shaky, then Marcia giggled and I giggled and finally we broke up completely and laughed 'til we thought we'd bust. Finally, the humming stopped — we calmed down and went on to play the rest of the scene as if nothing had happened."

Junior smiled and said, "It's funny, all right, but I can't see it happening on the concert stage." (Junior was a very serious young man.)

"I'll never forget how you got back at Barry when you were playing *The Yellow Ticket*," Ralph laughed.

I joined in the reminiscence. "The idea hit me at the first rehearsal. You see, Junior, the leading man, Barry, was playing a Chinese Mandarin who grows old during the course of the play. He finally dies sitting center stage in a chair built like a throne. His arms are resting on the arms of the chair and his death is almost imperceptible. He stares open eyed at the audience, and they finally realize he's gone. At that point I come on in a long, flowing Chinese gown. I play his trusted manservant who has grown old with him through the years. My business was to come over to him, see that he was dead, bow my head in sadness, fold my hands into the sleeves of my gown and walk solemnly off stage. That's the end of the play.

"Well, on closing night I hid a lily in my sleeve, and I walked directly in front of Barry so the audience could not see what I was doing. I planted the lily in Barry's upturned fist and started walking to the wings. Barry tried to keep a straight face, but before I got halfway off, the 'corpse' let out a loud guffaw which was hardly heard because the audience was laughing along with him."

"Gee, I wish I'd been there," said Junior. "I could have played 'Caprice Chinois' as background music." (That kid had a one-track mind.)

Just before we reached New York, Ralph recounted a little game that I hadn't been aware of. It seemed Barry played a little game with himself. After each performance when he'd removed all of his costume and only his jockstrap remained, he would let it drop to one foot and then try to kick it off so that it would land on a peg just to the right of the door. He was successful in making it stay on the peg about half the time.

From time to time Ralph had received small loans from the local banker who was a regular patron of the theatre. He'd always paid them back in time, but later, when rumors of Ralph's difficulties in the candy business were heard, he'd been turned down cold. He wanted another opportunity to talk to the banker and was glad to see that this was the night of that worthy's regular appearance at the theatre. So, when the play was over and the banker raved over the leading man's performance, he asked him out for a cup of coffee, and surprisingly, the banker accepted—but said that first he'd have to stop backstage and congratulate Barry on his performance. Everything was right but the timing—because as the banker entered the dressing room he was hit in the face with a jockstrap. That was the wrong time for Barry to miss.

"Pennsylvania Station!"

The porter handed us our bags as we alighted from the train.

It had been agreed that Ralph and Junior would go to my mother's place and deposit Junior and their bags while we took the fateful trip to the Long Beach crap game. Now we lugged our baggage (to save tipping a porter) through the long tunnel which led from the railroad part of Penn Station to the I.R.I. subway section that bore the same name. From then on it was easy. A nickel in the turnstile and we got on the uptown express. It was only three stops to our destination — 42nd Street, 72nd Street and 96th Street. We then walked the three blocks to 2626 Broadway.

There were tears in her eyes as my mom threw her arms around me. We had never been separated for so long a period and she was joyful that her boy was home. Because Mom and I had exchanged letters at least once a week she knew everything that had transpired in Oklahoma City. So after commiserating with Ralph and Junior she showed the three of us through the apartment and turned over a bedroom to the Roses insisting that they at least spend the night.

Junior asked, "Mrs. Bergman, would it be alright if I practiced?"

"Why of course, young man. After all the raves I heard from Teddy, it'll be a pleasure for me to listen. But I think it would be better if you do it in the kitchen. That way we'll be farthest away from my brother's office. We wouldn't want his drilling teeth to bother you."

"Mom," I said, "give me a kiss and wish us luck. Ralph and I are going out on a little business matter. We'll be back early but we'll eat out, so don't make dinner for us."

"Alright, Teddy." She kissed me and again the tears. "Oh, I'm so glad you're home, boychick!"

With that, we were off. Now it was back to the huge Pennsylvania Railroad Station, but this time to the Long Island division. Long Beach was an hour's ride on the express. I knew the beautiful seaside resort because I'd worked as a busboy at the Hotel Nassau one summer during the school holiday. So now, as planned, we went to the hotel where the crap game was held (not The Nassau) and had dinner in the dining room. I had tried once to get into the game, but the guy at the cubbyhole had said, "Unh-uh ... you're too young." I had shown him a twenty dollar bill and the guy laughed and said, "Come back when you're twenty-one and can show us five hundred in cash, that's the minimum here!"

So after dinner we casually went down to the basement and knocked on the door. The voice behind the screened cubbyhole said, "Whaddaya want?"

"We wanna play," I answered.

"Oh yeah? How old are ya?"

"Twenty-one," I said (I was actually nineteen).

"Let's see yer five C's."

I showed him.

"Okay, come on in."

The door opened and we were in what must have been a store-room — no furniture, just one big oblong table in the middle of the joint — and I do mean joint. The floors creaked, the plaster was coming off the walls — it was awful.

It was early. There were only about fourteen guys around the crap table. They'd be crowded three deep later on. The table had no markings on it; it was rough wood with four raised sides. The dice had to hit the farthest wall or the roll didn't count. Also, if one or both dice bounced off the table, the roll was no good and had to be done over. And, unlike the Vegas games of today, the players bet each other and paid the "house" a fee for the privilege. The house also collected a dollar from each new roller and another dollar for every pass (win) he made. The only time the house would bet was when a player couldn't get his wager covered. The house would then cover the balance and charge 5% for doing so. Needless to say this was most remunerative for the "unknowns" who ran the game. However, the game had gone on for so long that everyone knew that high officials of the succeeding city administrations were getting a helluva slice. The chief job of the house man was to see that nobody slipped in a pair of phony dice. The game was on the up and up.

I knew the odds but luck was against me on the first few wagers I made. By the time the dice got around to me, all that was left was $175. Then... as Ralph told it:

"It was like a miracle! *Somebody* wanted me to open that store... wanted Teddy to go to the American Academy of Dramatic Arts! Right off the bat... Seven! Next roll... "Eleven! In short, Teddy made seven passes (winning wagers) and we walked away from the table winning $2,800."

We floated home in a joyful daze. When we got there I grabbed my mother off her feet and whirled her around amid squeals.

"Put me down… What happened? You struck a gold mine?"

"That we did, mom — that we did!"

I laughed exuberantly, as I sat down in a chair and put $1,000 in her lap.

"Ach, Teddy… you gambled… you promised me…"

"This was the big one, Mom. We had to take a chance."

And I told her of Ralph's and my plans.

CHAPTER 3

The Village Life

The American Academy of Dramatic Arts was at that time the most prestigious drama school in the country. It was situated in the Carnegie Hall building at 57th Street. I was a bit nervous as I informed the young lady at the desk of my desire to enroll and she gave me a rather lengthy application form.

"When you've finished this," she explained, "it will be passed on to Dr. Jellinger and we'll inform you when you're to audition."

I thanked her. "Got any ideas of what kind of material would be right for the audition?"

The receptionist smiled. "Anything you feel comfortable doing. Dr. Jellinger just wants to hear your voice and get an idea of your ability."

"One more question," I said. "What is the cost if I'm accepted?"

"The basic course is one year, divided into two semesters. You must pass the first semester or you'll be dropped. The charge is $600 per semester, and it can be paid $100 a month if you'd rather."

This sounded good to me, so I filled out the application and two days later I auditioned for Dr. Jellinger — and was accepted. My class would begin the following Monday. I paid the first month's tuition and went home to tell the good news to Mom.

In the meantime Ralph had had a piece of luck practically fall into his lap. As he and Junior left the apartment their first morning in New York he noticed a big sign in a store in the same building:

GOING OUT OF BUSINESS!
EVERYTHING ON SALE
50% OFF

Thinking it was just another con game to get rid of excess merchandise, he and Junior went on their way to see Professor Auer.

However, Ralph thought on the way downtown that the neighborhood would be ideal for the kind of candy store he had in mind. All of his chocolate would be hand-dipped right in front of the passersby. He would have a huge copper vat in the window and the public could see and smell the candy specialties as they were being made.

Leopold Auer was gracious. He listened attentively while Junior expertly played *Symphony Espanol* by Lallo. When it was over, Auer said, "My poy, you play beautifully, vay beyond your years. Unter ordinary zeercoomstahnces I vould lof to teach you. But alahs, I am now old und zick unt I must leaf next viik for Pahden-Pahden for my health. I am afraid, my poy, zat my teachink days are ofer."

"Oh, Professor Auer, we are terribly sorry to hear that! What terrible news for all lovers of music," sympathized Ralph. "Let us hope the baths at Baden-Baden restore you to health."

"Sank you. Zat's very kind of you, but ven vun gets pahst eighty, it's time he moofed azide. But nefer mind me — your zon's talent iss too great not to insure zat he gets proper development. Zere iss a fine school viz very dedicated and capable teachers zat I will recommend. It is called Ze Julliard School. I vill gif you a letter to ze principal und I am sure zey vill accept him. He vill be in goot hands."

"Thank you!" echoed Ralph and Junior simultaneously.

The endorsement from Professor Auer saw Ralph Rose Jr. enrolled in the great Julliard School of Music. Ralph's mind was at rest. He could now pursue his immediate problem without concern. So when they got back to 2626 Broadway he and Junior dropped into the delicatessen next door to the "Going Out of Business" place, sat at one of the small tables and ordered a couple of corned beef sandwiches and celery tonics. He also asked the proprietor if he thought the sale next door was a legitimate one.

"Unfortunately yes," answered the kindly delicatessen owner.

The man who owned it had passed away the previous week and his wife was trying to salvage what she could from the business. He had been an expert tailor and had a small bit of haberdashery which was now practically sold out. She'd probably close up the following week.

Ralph asked him who the landlord was, and by that afternoon had negotiated a lease and "The Southern Rose Candy Shop" was launched. He could take possession on the tenth of the following month. So the Roses stayed on with us while I started my dramatic schooling and Ralph began gathering supplies and fixtures for his business.

The first month at the Academy did not live up to my expectations. I had the feeling that Dr. Zellinger's method was wrong, for the simple reason that every one of the twenty-two people in the class was being taught the same thing with no regard for the individuality of the varying would-be performers. In all fairness, as I had to admit in later years, one month was not a fair trial, and as year after year the school turned out many people of great talent, I conceded that I had been premature in my judgment.

During that month I did learn some important "Don'ts" which stood me in good stead in the years to come. But with the impetuosity of youth, I quit the school feeling I'd do better with practical experience in the New York theatre. However, the New York theatre wasn't exactly waiting breathlessly for the arrival of Teddy Bergman! I joined the gang of young out-of-work actors at Walgreen's Drug Store. I made the rounds of producers and agents. Chamberlain Brown sent me on one interview — nothing. It was a sad letdown to my dream of conquering Broadway.

While I was experiencing failure, Ralph was having great success with his store. The fragrant odors pouring out into Broadway made passersby stop and look at Ralph in a chef's hat making one delicious batch of candy after another in the window. He couldn't make enough of his Pecan Pralines.

I observed all of this and got an idea. A new item had been introduced to the American public that year — it was called cellophane. I thought if Ralph could package the pralines in this wonderful see-through material and put a gold stamp on the back to hold it together, it could be a winner on the wholesale market. Ralph liked the idea and we formed a separate company, each putting up half of the money which reduced my savings to a very low point. We began small. We bought an old Model T Ford which Ralph taught me to drive and I went out to sell all over the city. At first I made sales only to small individually owned candy stores and a few drug stores. The item was a great success. Then I tried some of the larger organizations. I sold to Huyler's, then a very deluxe chain. As repeat orders kept coming in, we had to rent the basement of a brownstone house on 99th Street. We eventually hired forty girls and more equipment to handle the business. The large chains were the Nedick's Orange Juice stands (over a thousand in the city), and the Union News Company, which had newspaper and candy stands in every subway in the five boroughs.

These orders, according to company rules, were sold on consignment only. However, these last accounts were selling 4,000 dozen pralines a week and kept paying their bills and constantly reordering.

Came the summer — and disaster!

The beautiful see-through packaging which had served to make the customers grab the pralines off the counter now had the opposite effect. The humid summer heat caused the sugar in the pralines to grain and the crisp-looking pecans softened into the white mess.

Overnight we were out of business — the entire investment lost.

This experience had different effects on our partnership. To me it had only been a stop gap in my theatrical career. I had thought I'd be able to add to my bankroll and then have another go at the theatre. So I was broke — so what? I'd just have to try harder. I'd make it!

But to Ralph the disaster became the climax to a growing period of discontent. He had once again found himself disenchanted with life in New York, and while his store was doing quite well, he longed for the simple life of Oklahoma. So he came to a hurried decision. He would bring Florence Rose, his ex-wife, east (if she'd come and she did), give her the store and he'd go back and start another store in Oklahoma City. This would assure Junior's continuance at Julliard with his mother to make a home for him. This he soon set in motion. He found a comfortable small apartment for them and before long, he was gone.

One day I received a tip from a friend at Walgreen's that a new theatre group was starting up at the Cherry Lane Theatre in Greenwich Village. We both lost no time in getting down there and we were both cast in small parts at $15 a week. Also starting at the same salary, but playing the lead, was a highly touted young actor just out of Cornell University with the unusual name of Franchot Tone. The play (*The Belt* by Paul Sifton) depicted the plight of the worker as his needs forced him into the monotony of turning a screw or applying a wrench to the passing automobiles. The company was called "The New Playwrights Theatre" and was funded by a $35,000 grant from Otto Kahn, the banker/philanthropist.

In addition to *The Belt*, we did *The Centuries* by Em Jo Basshe, *International* by John Howard Lawson, and *Airways, Inc.* by John Dos Passos. George Tobias, my friend from Walgreen's, and I were cast in all four shows. In the last play of the season I took on the job of stage manager and got an extra five dollars a week. This was enough to rent a room on Commerce Street and once again I left home. My mother didn't like it, but she recognized my need and acquiesced.

Now a whole new vista opened for me — the Village Life. During the day George and I would wander through Little Italy (Bleeker Street), Chinatown (Mott and Pell), to some small out-of-the-way eating places in alleys, sampling foods that I had never known existed. George's mother, Madam Tobias, was a big star in the then very prosperous Yiddish Theatre and George had had the where-withal to indulge his gourmet tastes. So I, whose mother had kept a kosher home, now found my appetite titillated by lasagna, chub choy, shrimp with lobster sauce, tempura, Sukiaki — and in one unusual place on the second floor of MacDougal Alley — tiny birds called Reed Birds. There were 24 to a portion, and all were browned to a crisp. They were so delicious — you ate the bones and all!

After the performances at night we indulged in heavier sport. It was the only time in my life which could be referred to as "my alcoholic period." There were two favorite spots — one, a wine cellar in a basement on MacDougal Street, where the stout Italian sold his homemade wine from barrels at ten cents a glass.

The only favorite haunt was a place called "Julius" — famous for its whiskey sours. It was at the juncture of Waverly Place and 10th Street. It had three entrances — one on 10th Street, one on the corner at Waverly Place, and a family entrance about 50 feet down the block on Waverly. There was a tale told by the bartender that probably had an element of truth in it. He claimed that one night a guy came in the 10th Street entrance stoned beyond speech, staggered up to the bar and said, "Risky Rower — wooshky woeer."

The bartender, seeing he'd had too much said, "Sorry, old timer. No more for you tonight!"

Very meekly the drunk lurched out the door, took a few steps and re-entered the corner entrance and went up to the bar, mouthed a few incoherencies that finally sounded like "Swooshky our — Soursky whisky!"

The bartender got stern. "Now look you, you're makin' a pest of yourself. You can't have anymore tonight. Now get out of her and stay out!"

Out went the drunk. By some miracle he negotiated the fifty feet down Waverly Place, entered the family entrance, only knocked over three chairs and a table on his way to the bar, and once again: "Wh-wh-whisky sur."

The bartender grabbed a bung starter and shouted, "Do you want me to bust this over your head? Now get out of here. Git! Git! Git!"

Very calmly the drunk looked at him and said, "Shay. D-d'you think you own all the bars in this neighborhood?"

True or not, the customers loved it.

Julius' bar was part of a ritual that George and I followed two nights a week. We'd have three hefty whisky sours, then, feeling no pain, we'd proceed to the Luxor Baths on 46th Street where for a dollar each we were given a cubbyhole with a cot to sleep on. We would then strip and go to the hot room (130 degrees) where we would wrestle on the rough mats. Both George and I were exceedingly strong and very evenly matched so that sometimes these bouts would last an hour. The next morning, despite the mat burns and bruises, we would be so full of the *joi de vivre* that it was hard holding us down.

It wasn't all play. The New Playwrights was the kind of theatre where everybody pitched in and did everything. My new duties as stage manager found me spending entire nights in the theatre, building and painting sets, cleaning and preparing the book for the next play to go into rehearsal. It was an exhilarating learning experience and I felt my decision to quit The Academy had been correct.

The New Playwrights Theatre lost its sponsor after the third production, *International* by John Howard Lawson. They had enough left to finish the first season, but they would have to give up the theatre and find a place to house what was to be their first production of the following season: *Singing Jail Birds* by the renowned Upton Sinclair. It was also their last.

During this period a young artist came to the company and volunteered to help design and paint scenery. He had been a seaman and had just returned from a seven-month journey around the world. Now he wanted to settle down and start painting. My remarkable physique led the artist to offer me $1.75 an hour to pose for him. I was glad to get this, so three days a week I went to the artist's one-room, sunlit studio, put on white face makeup, got into white tights and shirt and posed for what in time would become a world-famous painting. It now hangs in the Metropolitan Museum of New York.

The title of the painting is "The White Clown." The artist was Walt Kuhn.

Kuhn, historically known today as having a key role in founding the Association of American Painters and Sculptors, is still revered for his specialty work of *commedia dell'arte*-style portraits of circus and vaudeville entertainers.

The White Clown painting by Walt Kuhn.

Alan's son, Alan Reed, Jr., recalled that "'The White Clown' was significant to Dad only because when, as a young man to earn a few extra bucks, he
sat as a model for a painting that became quite valuable and was by an artist
who became quite well known. Pure happenstance. His appreciation of art
was mostly in *objets d'arte* — carvings, figurines, furniture."

This period of time also saw the awakening of political consciousness in me. I began to perceive the differences in the ongoing battle of Right and Left. Because the New Playwrights were solidly of the Left, my thinking was undoubtedly influenced by them. With my natural tendencies leaning toward the defending of the underdog I was a prime prospect for my boss' subtle instructions. It took many years of perception of the various gradations within both Right and Left to bring me to my final political conclusion. I was and am a Liberal Democrat.

There were humorous happenings that began pointing out some of the ludicrous aspects of the Far Left. All of the members of the company were "advised" that it would be "good business" if they would patronize an eating place called The Proletcos Cafeteria. The reason it was described as "good business" was that the main source of income for the theatre was from union buyouts of the entire 300-seat Cherry Lane. Inasmuch as many of the Union bosses hung out at the Proletcos it would be good for the company to be seen there. This made sense to me, and I went to the cafeteria as much as possible.

Very often, when a Union would buy out the house, a lot of imbibing of alcohol took place. One night during the run of *The Centuries*, a guy out front was feeling no pain. In the play I was portraying a rabbi who had grown old. The building where I had my synagogue was being demolished, and I was wandering about the stage half crazed, saying, "My children have all left me. Some have gone to Harlem, some to the Bronx. Where shall I go? Where shall I go?"

At which point our inebriated critic out front spoke up. In a loud voice, he declaimed, "Go to hell. You stink!"

I looked at him, nodded my head and left the stage as the curtain came down. That was true audience involvement.

The Playwrights found a home for *Singing Jail Birds* at the Provincetown Theatre on MacDougal Street. The Provincetown was a converted stable. It could hold an audience of 200 by squeezing. It was also the home of a famous theatrical happening that had occurred the season before. Eugene O'Neill's *Emperor Jones* was being presented with Charles Gilpin in the title role and Moss Hart as the Cockney trader. The play opened to the sound of jungle drums. Gilpin's first line was "Ya hear dem drums?"

On opening night Gilpin had consumed a lot of whisky to help his first night jitters. He was kind of floating as the curtain parted — and he chose that moment to break wind with such a resounding bombardment that it was heard perfectly by the last seat in the last row. Without batting an eye he said to Moss Hart, "You hear dem drums?"

The flustered future playwright could only reply, "Y — y — yes."

And Gilpin said, "Well, you're gonna hear 'em again!"

And hear 'em the audience did, as a second huge rumble blasted forth from the relieved "Emperor."

Singing Jail Birds had a good run at the Provincetown, but did not make enough to warrant a second full season without a sponsor. Everyone was given two weeks notice and The New Playwrights Theatre came to an end.

But for me it was a beginning. Self-salesman that I was, I had ingratiated myself with the Provincetown management. I was hired to act in and manage their next production — E. E. Cummings' *Him*. My salary: $40 per week. The second act of *Him* was a dream sequence that had nine separate scenes. I was cast in three of these roles and Lionel Stander, George Bratt and Stanley Zipser played in the others. One Saturday matinee neither Stander nor Zipser showed up at the theatre and Bratt and I had to do all nine scenes between us. It was bedlam! Such a putting on and taking off of crepe hair, wigs and makeup — with me having the additional task, as stage manager, of pulling curtains, setting up props and making offstage sound effects. Finally the nightmare came to an end. Just as I was exhaustedly leaving the theatre for a bit of food between shows, Stander and Zipser strolled calmly in. Their excuse — they thought it was Friday and only had one show to do at night! Rather than recast that late in the run they were let off with a strong reprimand from management and allowed to continue. I often wondered what powerful sedative could cause one to lose a whole day.

The next production at Provincetown had no acting role for me but I remained as stage manager. This particular play introduced a very young lady who was to make theatrical history and reach the very pinnacle of stardom. She was making her professional debut having just graduated from John Murray Anderson's School of Theatre Arts. Her name? Bette Davis!

I now felt I was ready for Broadway and I began frequenting the downstairs coffee shop at Walgreen's getting the latest scuttlebutt on what producers were casting, etc. I learned of a young, new producer called Chester Erskine who was then casting a play called *The Last Mile*. Wonder of wonders, at Erskine's office I was given a chance to read for one of the leading roles. I was called back three times to read with other people and I thought I was in. But, alas, I was unsophisticated as to salaries for Broadway productions, and when asked what salary I expected to be paid for the role, I gulped and said, "$75 a week."

I had never earned more than the $50 that Ralph had paid me and did not know that the smallest bits were paid around $125 a week and leading roles much more. I was being considered for the part of "Killer Mears," a great acting opportunity. I often reflected in later years on the fact that had I had enough guts to ask a much higher price, my career might have taken a different course. I felt that my naiveté caused the producer to realize my inexperience and engage another actor. The play went on to become a solid hit and the actor who played "Killer Mears" and later repeated the role in the successful movie version of *The Last Mile* was to become another of the brightest stars in theatrical history — Spencer Tracy!

Now I was faced with a long summer time of no work. I heard through the grapevine of a place called Camp Copake and its owner Sam Zasuly. I applied for a job on the social staff and, due to my muscular physique, was engaged as Physical Director at $200 for the four-month season plus room and board. It was to become a great learning experience, an opportunity to spread my wings in many directions.

It's a shame that three chapters are as far as Alan went with his life's story. He did outline what would come, hoping to get a publisher interested enough to say, *please write more*. But the outlines were never fleshed out.

CHAPTER FOUR

Life at Camp Copake in the Berkshires

This chapter will introduce new experiences for me that will contribute to my ever-growing interest in all phases of entertainment. A resident at Copake was Jaques Wolfe, head of the New York Conservatory of Music. I was given a bungalow by Sam Zasuly, the owner. This was in exchange for Jaques' bringing a select group of his advanced instrumentalists who acted as caddies on the golf course during the day and joined with the regular 18-piece orchestra for a 63-piece symphony under the stars each Thursday evening. I was the Master of Ceremonies for these events, thereby getting my first good experience with music.

It was at Copake that Jaques Wolfe composed "Glory Road" and "Shortnin' Bread" and where each had its first public performance. This chapter will also introduce Moss Hart as a young man struggling with his first play, *Once in a Lifetime*, and will tell a very heartwarming experience shared by Moss and myself.

The chapter will include much humor built around adult camp life, and will introduce Charlie Wight who became my best friend. He was a fellow actor, very talented, with a fine mind. He would become my political mentor.

Toward the end of the chapter we will meet Herb Polesi, a guest at the camp, who will be responsible for my breaking into the new field of radio broadcasting.

Alan Reed, Jr. recalled that *"I always knew Dad loved his time at Copake Country Club and remembered it as a defining moment in his life. His interaction with creative people, many of whom became well known, informed much of his thinking and the kinds of things he appreciated in life.*

"*Several years ago my wife and I were on a driving trip in New England and found ourselves in upstate New York. As on a mission, we searched for and finally found the Copake Country Club. It was a rather modest golf club, as such places go, and I asked if there might be anything still around from the club's early days. The counter clerk, the only person there at the time, took us to an old storeroom and told us to look around. After much rummaging I spotted a faded black & white photo enlarged on a poster board. It showed four men standing on a golf course smiling to the camera. Among them was my father, some years after his apprenticeship there. Imprinted across the photo were words proclaiming the Annual Alan Reed Golf Tournament.*"

Eureka! Hidden gold. I wanted so badly to take it, especially since it would just continue to gather dust there. But the clerk, without authority, couldn't allow it. I did manage to snap a picture of it, however, and couldn't wait to get home to show it to my mom."

CHAPTER 5
Radio

This will be a summary of my 25 years in radio from the early beginnings of the industry to its demise as popular entertainment. It will be full of anecdotes connected with my rise in this new medium and will show why Teddy Bergman became Alan Reed.

It will cover the less disciplined early days and show the gradual approach to what Hal Kantor, the great wit and writer, called "The Theatre of the Mind" and television "the Theatre of the Mindless."

It will show through both anecdote and history my close association with many of the creative people in the industry: Fred Allen, Eddie Cantor, Al Jolson, Fanny Brice, David Freedman (the master writer of comedy), Bert Lahr, Jimmy Durante, Jack Benny, Ed Gardner of *Duffy's Tavern* — you name it, I was in the middle of it, both in New York and Hollywood. It will show me along with Charlie White and George Heller as the founders of The American Federation of Radio Actors. It will contain a sidelight of television experimentation by CBS in 1931 which resulted in my marriage to the beautiful singer, Finette Walker. It will show how Hollywood grew to eventually having more national programming than New York. It will also show a group of top radio stars who fell by the wayside when Television began gobbling up the best of Radio and Motion Pictures, to the detriment of both. It will carry a small group of central characters who were able to perform in any medium. It will touch on the blacklisting — the period of the "Hollywood Ten" and its effect on me and my friends and co-workers — multi-talented people who had to take any kind of job to survive.

Out of this chapter (it is hoped) will come a clearer understanding of the constant battle between the creative people and those who control the purse strings.

Alan spoke about his radio days extensively with Chuck Schaden, producer and host of the long-running radio program, *Those Were the Days.*

"We met on February 17, 1975," wrote Schaden in his interview book, *Speaking of Radio,* "in his large, rambling ranch-type home, tucked away in a beautiful residential corner of Hollywood, California."

That interview is reproduced, with kind permission, here.

When did you first get involved with radio?

It was 1926. I had been working at a summer place called Copake. It's still in existence in New York State. It was an adult camp. From this place emerged a great many, many people: Moss Hart, for instance; Jacques Wolfe, who wrote "Shortnin' Bread" in the glory days. Mischa Auer, George Tobias, myself, a great many people were on the staff of this place. A guest came up the summer when I was 19, and talked about working for the Judson Radio Program Corporation. He told me that they were doing all of the radio programs for the networks. This was a newly formed subsidiary of the Judson Concert Bureau, which is the largest booking company of concert attractions. He told me [to come] up to his office in New York. He was a kid [and it] turned out he was an office boy up there, but he was learning the business. His name was Herb Polesi, who later on had *Twenty Questions.* Later on we did a program together called *Henry and George* for Henry George Cigars. He introduced me to [Hazel] the secretary of Charlie Skank, who was the producer [of] *True Detective Mysteries, My True Story, Physical Culture,* all [based on] the Bernarr McFadden magazines. They had an exclusive on the stories in them.

He introduced me to [Skank's] secretary, who took a look at my youthful face and said, "He has only one part open this week, and that's of a head mobster and I'm afraid you're too young for that. All the rest of the parts are cast." It was around lunchtime and I waited for her to go out to lunch, and I saw her go out to lunch, and I went into Herb's office and got the phone and asked for Charlie Skank, who was in the other office. He got on the phone and I said, "Hellow, Skank, uh…" He said, "Who is this?" I said, "Never mind who this is. I'm just gonna tell you somethin'. I'm comin' into your office in a couple of minutes. You're gonna give me a job, or you're goin' for a ride. You understand?" He said, "What the hell! Who is — come in here!" So, I went in there and got the job! That was the beginning of radio. I had done one thing before that. I'd been with a group in the Village called The New Playwrights Theatre. We, as a semi-professional group, met in competition with a supposedly amateur group of radio actors that WOR had. We each presented a play. It was a phony set-up publicity contest, but that was the first time. This was the first time I got paid.

Well, it's a good time to remember, then.

My Darling!
It is you who make
me smile. I shall always
love you.
Teddy

Yes! Well, from then on, Charlie and I became very good friends. I worked all of the shows and got a good, firm, early footing in the radio business. Because very shortly, the radio business emerged to the place where knowledge and quickness were very important to the director. He didn't have time to stop and teach a guy how to read a line, or what to do, because you're always fighting a time thing. So I was in at the beginning and got the experience, and by the time radio started to get really big, I was there and working like mad.

You were quite versatile and able to do all different kinds of voices. That was invaluable before the union days, when you could double and triple and all that.

Yes, true, true, true. I'm one of the founders of the union. I don't know if you knew that. There were three of us: George Heller and John Brown and myself, and we belonged to the Forum in Equity. We sat down and we started talking of the need for a union. By this time, there were a lot of people working, but in radio, from the beginning to the end, there was like a hierarchy. Maybe 90 per cent of the work was done by 10 per cent of the people. Of that 10 per cent of the people, maybe 10 per cent were always going. It was due to the early stock [companies] and friendships that were formed, and knowledge of the business. Everybody threw his hand in those days in many varying things. For instance, I was on one of the phones at CBS where I was working mostly then, when Orson Welles had his "War of the Worlds" thing, and everybody was at a phone answering calls. It was frantic! It was frightening.

People were really taken in by that.

Oh, it was so believable, they were frightened, really frightened. People were calling.

What did Welles think about that?

At the time, he didn't think about it, but it certainly caused a lot of new directions in the radio business. They had to be informed, if there was even a remote possibility of anybody getting frightened, that this was a radio broadcast. It was not real. It was a strange, strange time in radio in those days.

Did you work most of the time in New York in those early days?

Yes, I worked in New York until 1943. Then out here ever since. Half my life there, half here. A lot of strange things happened in the early days. The soap operas were like a factory [with stories] that were being turned out. The same writers would be engaged to write two shows at once, so that you would find plots that you were playing on one show, were also running with different names on another show. Now, I did *Big Sister* and *Myrt and Marge* back to back. One was on from 10:00 to 10:15, and the other was on 10:15 to 10:30. I would just walk across the studio, you know, into the other room. I played heavies for two years straight on both of these. One, [heavy] was called Asa Griffin and the other [heavy] was called something like Zefferini or something…a hardnosed gangster. Asa Griffin was seemingly a kindly old man who was a horror! He burned down orphanages for personal gain. He did all kinds of things. And the same bloody plots were occurring back and forth all the time!

In those early days, they tried to get the sponsor's name involved in these things. Like Myrt and Marge were Myrtle Spear and Marjorie Minter, sponsored by Wrigley's Spearmint gum.

Myrt and Marge! I mentioned before that Herb Polesi and I did *Henry and George.* We were plugging the Henry George Cigars. We played characters called Henry and George (I was George), and we had an orchestra, and a male singer and a female singer on the show. We were like traveling bellhops. Later on, Major Bowes went to cities and told about the city. We had the same thing. Never left the studio, of course. We told all about what was happening in Detroit, Minneapolis, Chicago and all around. There'd be one-minute blackouts, then there'd be a musical number, and it was for Henry George Cigars. [Our theme song was: "You can all afford a Henry George, so smoke your troubles away. With the smoke rings disappearing, cloudy skies will soon be nearing." I've never forgotten that!]

And you were on a program called Harv and Esther.

Right. And it was the same company. I'll tell you, there is a very interesting tale connected with that. *Harv and Esther* was for Harvester Cigars. [The series ran from September 12, 1935 to March 5, 1936 for CBS on Thursday nights at 8, co-starring Audrey Marsh as Esther.] The Consolidated Cigar Company was the owner of both the previous *Henry and George* and *Harv and Esther*. They were related to the Paleys. The Paleys made the La Palina Cigars. Now, there was some connection, and I don't remember what it was now, between Consolidated Cigar Company and Paley, who founded the CBS Network. But, I had been doing *Henry and George* for three years. I got $50 a show the first year, and $100 a show the second year, and $150 the third year. This was a lot of dough for me. This was a time when you were kids, and that money meant a lot more than today.

I went to a party one night, and a little man came up to me. He said, "I'd like to introduce myself. My name is Lichtenstein. You're a young fella. I'm surprised we're paying you so much money."

I said, "Well, I appreciate what you're paying me, but 'so much money?' It's not that much."

He said, "A boy your age? You're making $750 a week."

I said, "What?" and I told him what I was getting. Judson Radio Program Corporation had been billing him for my services at $250, $500, and $750. I was getting $50, and $100 and $150.

Well, this kind man got on the phone the next day to Judson, and raised Holy Cain with them. He said, "If you ever want to do business with me again, you will adjust that for that nice young man I met last night."

I got a check for $12,500. And it was fantastic!

Oh!! When was this, about what year?

1930. Not many taxes then, either.

Oh, boy!

Incidentally, in the beginning, when I started, what turned into CBS Network was originally station WABC in New York. They rented two hours of time from WOR and used their own call letters, WABC, while their station was being readied. Very few people know that. That's part of the history of the business. Paley had come up with his father's cigar money, and they owned a radio station down there, WCAU [Philadelphia]. They decided that they were going to see if they couldn't build another network, which they did. A pretty good one.

I want to tell you something that happened in 1931 and '32. Columbia, or CBS, was experimenting with television in their building at 485 Madison

How Alan made his entrance for Col. Stoopnagle, 1941.

Avenue. On the 23rd floor they had a tiny studio, and in those days, television was done with something that looked very much like a make-up mirror. Just a string of strong lights in back of which was the camera. Well, Stoopnagle and Budd and myself were waiting to go up and ad-lib. They asked everybody working at CBS to come up and do a stint. There were then 43 sets in New York. They were all close channel, you know, in advertising agencies and in a few [wealthy] homes.

Anyway, we're waiting to go on, and on the [television] receiver in the lobby, in this very small place, a girl was singing, a beautiful girl. She came out just as we were ready to go on, and I followed her. I said, "Can you wait downstairs? I want to talk to you." I wanted to make a date with her. She was gorgeous! So, Stoopnagle and Budd and I went in and we ad-libbed our way through [our routine]. We went downstairs, with the result that I asked the girl out for dinner. When we went across to a drugstore, which was on the street, we had dinner at the counter. I took her home, and that night I met her mother, who happened to be visiting New York. (They were from Washington.) Six months later we were married, and we've been married ever since. That was probably the first television romance. We now have our 43rd anniversary, and we have three children, boys, they've all married and we have 10 grandchildren.

Signing autographs with Col. Stoopnagle.

You were the voice of Falstaff Openshaw on The Fred Allen Show for years and years.

Before Fred Allen there were many things. I did straight for a lot of the comedians. I worked for David Freedman, who had a comedy factory. He had Fanny Brice, Eddie Cantor, Block and Sully, Burns and Allen. Every comedy act that was in New York, David Freedman supplied the material for. Again, the same jokes in different dialects! Jokes all around the place. I did the voice of Rubinoff on the Eddie Cantor show. Rubinoff never wanted to talk. He was frightened. Once he went to Pittsburgh. His home, union local was there and they were giving a big benefit. They invited Rubinoff and his violin — a radio benefit, you know — for the musicians. Eddie bet him $100 that he wouldn't open his mouth that he would just play his violin, because he was afraid to talk. He was a little embarrassed about his accent, but he shouldn't have been. He got on the air, was introduced by the master of ceremonies, "Rubinoff and his Violin," and he talked. All he said was, "Eddie Camphor owe me 100 dollar."

Well, when you were his voice on the Cantor show, did you do it with a Russian accent?

Oh, sure. Just as I sounded now. "Eddie Camphor, vhat's da matter vit you?" We had Rubinoff's wife. We had Rubinoff's everybody on the show. We played all kinds of things. I found a Russian accent once. I was driving in a cab in New York, and the cab driver turned around. I told him where I wanted to go.

He said, "I will inform you, sir, that you have the honor of being driven by a genuine Russian baron."

So I said, "Keep driving." We drove around Central Park and I picked this thing up, but he was quite a character. Dialects have always been kind of a specialty of mine.

When you were in radio you were using the name Teddy Bergman.

Which was my name. It was my father's name. I'll tell you how the name change came about. That happened in 1939. I changed it because by that time I was the busiest what we called, in those days, *stooge* in radio. I worked all of the comedy programs. [One of which, in 1939, was a five-minute NBC series called *Pipe Dreams*.] Every time I wanted to get to do a dramatic program, which I was proficient at, because I had some theatre before radio, the guys would say, "Ah, all you funny fellows, you want to act." I did want to act, and I couldn't get to first base. So, I decided, the dickens with this, I'm going to become a whole new person.

So, I changed my name, changed my manner of approach. I kept very few of the comedy shows, and just started on dramatic shows. By that time Stoopnagle's partner, Budd, had phased out of the picture. It became Stoopnagle and Reed. We had a show for a couple of years for Mennen's Skin Products. I was his announcer and partner and straight man, in effect, you see. So, I was able to create a whole new image and I wanted a name. I found Alan Reed. Reed was a family name of my wife's. Not her last name. Her father's name was Myron Reed Walker; his mother's maiden name was Reed. We had called our first-born son Alan Reed Bergman. I started looking around and there it was right in front of us. It's an awfully good name. I just chopped off the Bergman. I've had it legally changed since 1939 and that was it. But, I used to have a program under the name of Bergman — Blubber Bergman. I was on for several years for Van Heusen Collars. [*The Blubber Bergman Show* had led to a difficulty of Alan securing more straight/dramatic roles.]

What kind of show was that?

Well, Blubber — it's hard to say this — I had done *Joe Palooka*...

You were *Joe Palooka.*

I was Joe Palooka. Joe Palooka was a very naive kind of a fella. A great big guy, [a punchy] kind of guy. I kept his basic thing for Blubber. We added energy. He was so full of vitality that sometimes he'd get tied up in himself, you see, and then he would even switch words around. He said, "I gotta be goin' now. Good-boo, good-bee, so-long!" You see, this kind of a comic character. He was a lovable character. I had a straight woman, Betty Garde, whose attitude toward Blubber was kind of like a big sister. It was very good. But he was in love with her, you know, and he'd make these pathetic love speeches and get no place. It was an interesting kind of a show. [The 15-minute series sponsored by Heinz only lasted from April 12 to August 16, 1932 on CBS.]

When were you Joe Palooka?

We got married on the strength of my contract with *Joe Palooka*. It was very early in '32. After that I did a Harry Hershfield program called *Meyer the Buyer* [based on Hershfield's comic strip *Abie the Agent*, the first 15-minute episode was heard on August 25, 1932 and began rolling out the soap opera-like series with Meyer Mizznick (Reed) and his wife, Irma (Adele Ronson) fighting the woes of business and family life during the Depression; Meyer finally "bought it" in November of 1932]. *Joe Palooka* — I had a long contract which was beautiful on paper. It went off after 16 weeks. The reason it went off — it was on for H.J. Heinz, the pickle people, you know. Mr. Heinz belonged to a very swank club in Pittsburgh. He used to come into the club for lunch and the guys would say, "Well, who're you fightin' this week, Joe?" They'd start ribbing him about the program. It didn't bother him so much, but it bothered his wife, who came around. She insisted that this was too low-brow, the prizefight field, for her pickles. She ended up with the Longines Symphony. So we were out of the picture.

How much influence did the sponsors exert on the programming in those days?

Everything in those days. It was different than now. Now the network controls it.

Yes. Well, there are very few shows that are totally sponsored by a single advertiser today.

Yeah, true. But the network has been able to dictate terms to sponsors even when there's only one sponsor. There are some. It's a monopoly, too much so in my opinion, because I am solely against the number of [TV] reruns that are being done. I think it's horrible what we are faced with. It used to be that there would be reruns for 13 weeks in the summer hiatus. And 39 weeks would be booked solid. Or 26 weeks with option for another 13, in the old radio days

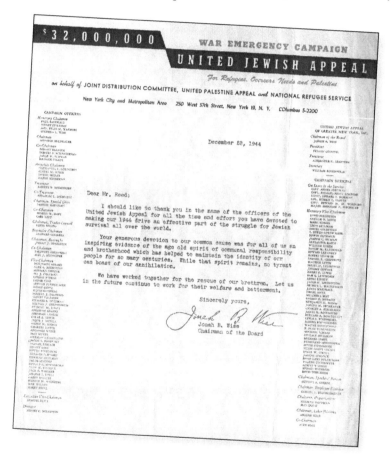

and on into television. Now we get nothing but rehashed stuff, and stuff that you've seen over and over and over again. This, of course, saves countless millions of dollars for the networks and an awful lot of effort having to put out new products. But, it also keeps an awful lot of actors out of work.

And it cheats the public, too, out of new stuff, something imaginative.

Of course it cheats the public. Of course it does. I don't know if you know this, but in the Screen Actors Guild, over 80 percent of our membership

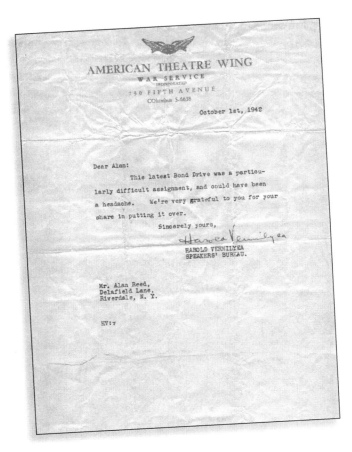

earn less than $2,000 a year. These are people who have made good money at some time, one time or another.

That may mean that they work in one TV movie, and that's it for the whole year.

Or 14 days at $100 a day--$120 or $130 — whatever it is now — the minimum. Who knows? Actors who would never take under a minimum of a week's contract are very happy to get day work. Thank the Lord *The Flintstones* has taken me out of that mess. I've been a very fortunate man.

You worked a number of years ago in radio with Mel Blanc on his show.

I was on Mel's show. Yes. He had his own show and I had my own show, and others — Hans Conried once had his own show. It is impossible for a good character man to come up with a central pleasing character that can carry a show. We've had to come to the realization that we belong in a certain spot. We are character men. We can play character leads, as we do in *The Flintstones*. But, in the old radio days, I had — you mentioned it — the Harvester show. I was the guy and I had top writers. But I never made it. Of course, I had tough opposition. I was on opposite Rudy Vallee and His Toppers. It was at its height.

Life With Luigi, on October 27, 1949 with Alan Reed (Pasquale), Hans Conreid (Schultz), Mary Shipp (Miss Spalding), J. Carrol Naish (Luigi), and Ken Peters (Olsen).

As a main character, a good solid supporting character in so many shows, you literally stole the show week after week.

In a lot of shows.

You were Pasquale in Life with Luigi.

Life with Luigi. That's a-right. You got-a memory! I loved that show. I like that more than any show I've ever done. That and with Fred [Allen]. Fred was an experience all in itself. Falstaff became a household word during the wartime period. On the strength of Falstaff, I did an awful lot of work in hospitals and canteens and things like that.

Didn't Falstaff open with a poem of some kind?

Yes, he'd knock on the door, and the door would open, and he'd say, "Blow the bugle. Toot the trumpet. It is Falstaff. Where shall I dump it?" And Fred would say, "Do you have a poem for us tonight?" He'd say, "Oh, indubitably. I might go so far as to say, in double-dubitably. Have you heard, 'Make for the Roundhouse, Nellie. The Brakeman Can't Corner You There'? or, 'She was a girl just down from Vancouver. He was a sailor bent on maneuver'?'

Fred would say, "Now wait a minute, Falstaff."

And then we would end up with a poem, about eight lines that would have relevance to the topic of the day in the Alley. It was a thing many people grew up with, as they've grown up with Flintstones.

Just about a month ago, along with a bunch of other radio people, we went up to Cal Arts University, which is the Disney-sponsored art school, full college upstate here, a little ways up. There were 21- and 22-year-olds. We addressed the Humanities class who were studying radio at the time of the Thirties. We did *Cisco Kid.* There were a lot of people who had worked in the original and who have since become personalities. First, we did *Cisco Kid* and I did Pancho, which was the thing that Mel did for a while. He replaced Harry Lang, who did it originally. "Hey, Cisco. What's the matter, Cisco?"

Later on, the master of ceremonies introduced each of us as what we're doing today, and when the guy mentioned Flintstone, it was amazing. It was like I was adopted by these people because they had grown up with it. They were just the right age in 1960, 15 years ago. They were seven years old, eight years old, six years old and they listened all through the years. Boy, the questions we were besieged with! It was an exciting experience.

You were on Abie's Irish Rose. *And there again, you almost stole the show. You were Solomon Levy, the father of Abie, right?*

Yes, Abie's father. That was one reason I couldn't come out here with Fanny Brice. Along about that time, I was the original Daddy to Fanny Brice's Baby Snooks.

Before Hanley Stafford?

Oh, we were in New York before Hanley even thought of doing it. We did it for about eight months. Then Fanny decided she had to come to the Coast and wanted me to come along with her. I couldn't. We had done, for two years before that, *Famous Lovers in History* in Yiddish dialect. We did Antony and Cleopatra, and Isabella and Columbus, imaginary things, which she wrote up and it was very funny. Fanny was very near-sighted, and she had her script done in very large type on special paper with a special machine.

Each page was on a cardboard, so that her script was this thick and she had a big podium. We knocked the podium down, and the script went all over the floor one show. I grabbed my mike and we're sorting out and ad-libbing. We did the whole program from the floor, with the audience sitting out there. That was a highlight. Fanny was a wonderful woman.

Abie's Irish Rose was fun. Menasha Skulnik was great on it. Everybody was great on it. Incidentally, Rosie was Mercedes McCambridge. She won an Academy Award. She was so great in *All the King's Men*. She came from Chicago and this was her first show in New York and she played Rose. It was a very cute show.

You were on The Shadow *for a while, weren't you?*

Yes, I played Shrevie, the cab driver, mostly, for a lot of years. [Specifically, in the "Love Story Drama/Love Story Hour" from October 1, 1931 to September 22, 1932.] There's an interesting tale about *The Shadow*. In the old days, getting personnel experienced in radio, which was a new medium, was rather difficult. So people would have to learn it from scratch. *The Shadow* was one of the earliest shows, not the earliest. Ruthrauff and Ryan was an agency that had come from a small office and one account — the Rinso account. It expanded into a huge organization. They had an awful lot of soap operas on and *The Shadow* was one of their shows. A fellow was put in charge, made supervisor of all daytime programs. He came up to Knight and Jordan. Knight and Jordan were the independent producers for Ruthrauff and Ryan of *The Shadow*. They both wrote and directed it, and hired and cast it. This guy came up to his office — Lamont Cranston was, of course, the Shadow. This great brain — I don't think he lasted much longer after this — came up and seriously sat down in their office and he said, "Now, I've been doing a lot of thinking, and I think that after this much time, you should develop a scene between Lamont Cranston and the Shadow. It would be very interesting." He had no idea what it was all about. He was in on the cuff, you know. There were a lot of people like that who had a brother-in-law or somebody and they just knew nothing.

Incidentally, in those days, there was no tape. There was just big, 16-inch records with 15 minutes on a side in those days. *Joe Palooka* was a 15-minute program, three times a week. If a mistake was made anywhere in the show, we had to start all over from the beginning. There was no snipping off a little bit and saying, "All right, pick it up from there." Frank Readick, who was the Shadow, incidentally, most of the time that I played it, played Knobby Walsh to my Joe Palooka. He had a tag line on the show, and he said, "Why, Joe will hit him with everything but the water bucket." That was the tag of the show. We get to the end of the show. We'd done pick-ups. We'd stopped two or three times, and we were exhausted. Now it was maybe the fifth time

Finette and the kids (seen more recently in a re-enacted photo on page 92).

we had gone over it. Finally, we get to the tag line and he said, "Joe is gonna hit him with everything but the gloves." And we were dead. We were dead!

And away you go, all over again!

Oh, yeah. It was bad.

Did you, on any of these broadcasts, have to do repeat shows for the West Coast?

On any of them? On *all* of them from New York. It's the chief reason I moved out here. I had a growing family, three little children. We lived in Riverdale in New York. I never got to see my family or have a meal with them more than once a month. The kids would be asleep. I'd get home late. By the time I'd get up, they'd be off to school. I had to get down early for the next morning because it was a long haul. I'd go from 9:00, 10:00 in the morning. My first show would be 10:00, sometimes earlier. I did one show that was on the air at 7:30. *Peggy Windsor's Letters*, we dramatized. There was an experience I had with that. We would rehearse that in the afternoon, and then come in at 7:30 in the morning. It was on NBC, and we'd do it. We would play all kinds of parts, background voices and everything. In the afternoon, they asked another fellow and myself if we'd play a couple of kids hollering good-bye [in high-pitched, kids' voices], "Good-bye, Daddy. Good-bye, Daddy." Well, we got in in the morning, and in the early morning voice, when I heard the thing it came out "Good-bye, Daddy" [in a low-pitched sleepless-night voice]. It was sickening. It was awful.

You were on My Friend Irma *for a while, weren't you, for a long while?*

Yes, I played her boss, Mr. Clyde. It was a fine experience. That and *Luigi* were on at the same time. As I said, *Luigi* was my favorite show.

He was, himself, a very lovable guy and you, as Pasquale, were always trying to marry off your daughter on the show, Rosa.

Yes, [Pasquale] was a villain with not too black a heart. But what I liked about the show was the sincerity of it. We approached it as if we were those people. In the orchestra — and this stands out in my mind as one of the rare life experiences — one of the orchestra men in our group was Italian and his father had never been out of Worcester, Mass., from the time he came over here. He had opened an Italian restaurant eventually in Worcester, Mass., and was there for lo all these years. *Life with Luigi* was a must. Serving stopped when the program went on. The big radio went on. Everybody had to listen to *Life with Luigi*. We kept getting reports and the son would read letters to us. Finally, he brought his father out to see the show. He was sitting in the first row. The man couldn't believe that he was seeing this. Tears were rolling down his eyes. I had all I could do to get through that program without breaking down because I realized what it had meant. If it meant that to him, I had realized that we had really succeeded in legitimacy, in believability. Both [J. Carrol] Naish and I were honored guests of the Italian American Society. It was an enjoyable experience.

The end of it was not enjoyable. The end of it — and this is to give you an idea of the times — the girl who played Rosa [Jody Gilbert] was called up before the Un-American Activities Committee. Instead of admitting that she had made a mistake, she raised hell and threw things around the place, and the sponsor took advantage of [the] moral turpitude clause and canceled the program. It cost me a quarter of a million dollars in both radio and television shows that we had going. We were just breaking into television. But, the aftermath of that, six months after it went off, the way times were and

J. Carroll Naish, Jody Gilbert and Alan Reed in *Life with Luigi*, 1949.

rumors got around, I went into a butcher shop that I frequented rather well. As the butcher was wrapping up my stuff he said, "Is it true that both you and Naish were canceled on the Luigi show because you're communists?" This is the way the thing happened. It was a frightening, frightening time.

Alan's son got in on the radio act, as well.

"With his help I started working as a child actor in radio. Occasionally we'd be on the same show together, and one humorous incident comes back to me. I was about fourteen or fifteen and we, along with seven or eight other actors, were on this week's edition of Lux Radio Theater. *By way of background to this occasion, I must tell you that Dad had narcolepsy, a sleeping disorder. His sleep patterns were very irregular and he could nod off at almost any time. Well, this was a live broadcast in front of a*

studio audience. For this series CBS used a theatre on Vine Street — separate from its regular studios at Sunset and Gower — that had a larger auditorium. (It later became a legit theatre known variously as the Huntington Hartford, the Doolittle, and now as the Ricardo Montalban.) So the microphones are set up near the footlights, the sound effects man is upstage in one corner with his gear, and all the cast members are seated in folding chairs behind the mikes with our scripts in hand. We would follow along and when our parts came near, stand and deliver. I'm sitting next to Dad and, as I see his part coming up, he's out like a light. A couple of nudges from me and he snaps back, just in time to avoid missing his cue. We laughed about it afterwards, and for the child I was, it was a fun story to tell.

"*As a child I had a knack for sight reading and doing characters, and I think that might have tickled Dad. Anyway, he was open to my interest in performing; he got me a wire recorder (before tape) and some sound effects records and I would write and produce little shows in my bedroom studio. Later, he made it possible for me to be on a couple of radio shows. That led to some semi-regular employment in those years, even though I stayed in regular school (not professional school for kids), which both parents insisted on. During high school and college I always assumed that when those days were over I would return to acting full time — which I did. Dad's advice to me was in the form of encouragement to follow my dream and to commit fully and with passion to whatever road I chose. I always loved putting shows together and produced some good-sized stage shows at Beverly and UCLA.*

"*When it came time to earn a living, I returned to acting full time, studying in workshops and with coaches — and before long I was working steadily. I felt so fortunate to be a part of Dad's profession and to have his blessing and encouragement.*"

The acting bug had been caught, but it wasn't a long-lasting disease.

"*Over a period of about twelve years I did a lot of TV shows, a few feature films, some legit theater, and a series of radio programs for AFRTS,*" he recalls. "*During this time I also produced and directed a couple of short films and some live theater. I made very little money from these ventures, but they allowed me to be happily engaged in one of my first loves. As my family started to grow I looked back over my career path and came to believe that my acting career had probably peaked and that I didn't want to spend the rest of my life pursuing jobs and having plenty of down time between them. I had become interested in the production of television and radio commercials and, with great good fortune, was able to transition into that field, where I stayed active for the next thirty years. So, in a sort of private sense, I never did give up show business. I often thought of the spots I produced as little movies.*"

The longevity of Alan Sr.'s radio career may well stem eternally from his time with Jack Benny's nemesis, Fred Allen. On Allen's program, Reed played the slightly effete, always-pompous Falstaff Openshaw, the Bard of Allen's

U. S. NAVAL AMPHIBIOUS TRAINING BASE
Solomons Branch
Washington, D. C.

Chaplain's Office
February 2, 1943

The Fred Allen Broadcast
N.B.C. New York City
New York

Dear Falstaff:

May I add my squeak to what I am sure
is an ever increasing cheer for your well-
turned words on last Sunday's program,
about "Eating out."

If I am a judge of true inspiration
and well worded sentiment I am sure you
have had a few-million copies printed.
May I have one?

Being the Chaplain at a very difficult
assignment where the men were told, in so
many words, that they were a suicide squad-
ron I voice the feelings and sentements of
all when I thank you for your humaness and
heartiness.

Respectfully yours

H. C. MacLeod
Chaplain

Alley. His cleverly bad poetry was heard weekly 'round the world. Still, at least the man was polite about his recitations; he always gave poor Fred Allen a choice before barging right in with the rhyming schmaltz.

> Falstaff: *Have you heard, "Oh to be a bobberlink, I'd sit and blink and wink and think?"*

Falstaff always recounted several titles he'd penned for his public, but many choices weren't good for Fred who was perpetually upset by the overblown poet's lack of judgment. Still, the owner of the show always allowed him to give out with at least one set of high-falutin' verbiage, such as "How Shall Falstaff Say Adeiu?" which was performed on June 28, 1942:

> *How shall Falstaff say adieu?*
> *"I'm frankly puzzled, entre nous."*
> *I know I could just say, "so long"*
> *but somehow "so long" sounds so wrong*

When the hyena parts with his hyena friends
he laughs farewell in glee
When a lion leaves his jungle mate
he roars goodbye to his she

The cobra hisses his parting words
the deer merely kisses his fawn
the skunk departing says nothing at all
everyone knows when it's gone

The little bee bumbles his bee adieu
the seal flaps goodbye in the sound
but I don't know how to leave you nice folks
so I'll just say, "I'll see you around."

On November 15, 1942 Openshaw gave Fred the following choices of his wacky rhyming:

"There We Were, Making Merry, She Sipped Her Foxy, I Munched My Cherry"
"When I Put the Turtle in Her Girdle, That's What Broke Up Me and Myrtle"
"Please Don't Interrupt, Judge — Let My Mother Finish Her Sentence"

And on other episodes:

"I have dedicated a new poem — to Hitler. 'If It Wasn't for a Gremlin, I Might've Reached the Kremlin."
"Said the Little Calf to the Big Giraffe, When I Look at Your Neck I Have to Laugh."

To help with the new can goods shortage during the war, on January 3, 1943, Openshaw released this epic to his brave public:

The World Needs One Big Can

I've been working day and night to perfect a mighty plan.
To me it's quite apparent that the world needs one big can.
If we all cut down on canned goods, the sooner the war we'll win,
the soldier can use the extra food, and Uncle Sam can save the tin.

And with that tin, Uncle Sam can call on every woman and man
to melt and mold and shape the tin to make the world one can.

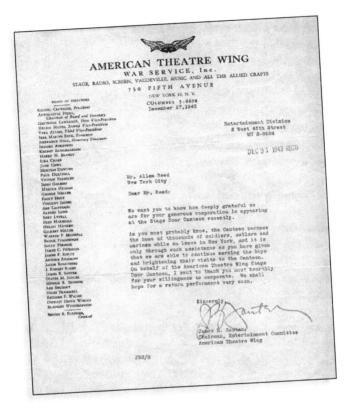

We can only use the biggest can, we can't use one that's littler
and when Uncle Sam has made it, he can tie that can to Hitler.

And when there was a fish shortage:

The Whale Called a Meeting

The big blue whale said, "A meeting, I decree,"
and he blew a spout that shook the sea.
The fish came in schools, the porpoises and seals
the flying fish flew, the crabs hitchhiked on eels

The minnows scurried, the haddock and sturgeon
joined the tuna and cod who needed no urgin'.
When all were assembled, from jellyfish to trout,
the whale said, "Here's what this meeting's about.

"Fish can't fight Hitler with guns or with powder
but we can give our lives for fish dinners and chowder.

Fish are like soldiers — for news we all pine
so to keep us both happy, please, drop us a line."

Those were the salad days that Alan remembered even through his television/*Flintstones* heyday. Alan was a *star* on *The Fred Allen Show*, and his happiness was not a retrospective emotion, as this letter (handwritten on Santa Fe, The Chief (train) stationery) bears out.

Tuesday – June 21 [1942]

Dear Fred,

At best my hand[writing] is damned near illegible, but when guided by the capricious movement of an extra fare train intent on earning its extra fare, I am sure the result will be more difficult to decipher than ancient Greek.

However I must risk it because I am impelled by a constant feeling of deep gratitude.

There are many things a guy can't say to another guy, face to face, that in a moment of calm reflection, he might be able to put down on paper.

First off, I want to say that I enjoyed a certain dignity while working for you, that I never had working for any other comedian. (As you know I've worked for them all.) For that I am appreciative.

Secondly, I have learned much from working for & with you & from watching you. You have improved my taste & judgment. For that I am appreciative.

And thirdly, your generous permission to use Falstaff. I can't help thinking how Cantor (not Charlie, the one with the sentiment) has reacted time and again in similar situations. Of course this is just another example of why you are held in such esteem in our profession.

I want you to know this, Fred. I am not a guy who forgets. I shall be eternally grateful, and if at any time, I can be of service to you in any way, it will afford me pleasure.

I know this letter sounds stilted as hell, but I've tried to tell you how I feel.

Please give my best to Porty [Fred's wife, Portland] and the gang, and believe me to be your appreciative friend

Alan Reed

[arrow points to name from:]
I've got to get used to that.

It seems the Fred Allen-created Falstaff character was so popular that Alan took it for his own *Falstaff Show* from April 3, 1944 to March 30, 1945. It was a 15-minute series for the Blue Network, broadcast Monday, Wednesday and Friday at 11p.m. Five years later, Alan and *son* joined forces on a five-minute children's show for ABC called *Falstaff's Fables*, which had a short run: September 18 to December 28, 1950.

Alan's son recalled how much Falstaff meant to his father.

"I'd be hard put to guess whether he had a favorite between Flintstone and Falstaff," he said. "Both were significant and rewarding roles at different ends of his career. He definitely identified with each during their time. He loved doing Falstaff and thought of Fred Allen as a great wit and good friend who was very generous. When Dad left 'Allen's Alley' in New York to pursue a career in Hollywood, Fred gave him carte blanche to do what he wished with the character of Falstaff Openshaw. Dad made numerous radio appearances through the years as Falstaff, guest shots on variety shows and on his own show for a while, and much enjoyed writing the ditties and doggerel (the shorter poems he called "puppyrel") along with his friend, writer Don Johnson. At one point in the late forties or early fifties he was asked by the Theater Guild to tour the country in a production of Shakespeare's 'The Merry Wives *of* Windsor, *starring Alan Reed as Sir John Falstaff.'"*

As Sir John Falstaff in *The Merry Wives of Windsor.*

East or West

It was Friday, April 30, 1943. I lived with my wife and three small sons in a charming house in Riverdale, New York. It was a serenely beautiful location... an acre and a half of lush foliage with a trickling, pebble-filled brook dividing our property and that of our nearest neighbor. He was a former United States Attorney General and had retired to 30 acres of rolling lawn that almost reached the Hudson River. With only the brook dividing our properties, it was as if this vast expanse of well-tended lawn was our own. Our vista was magnificent. We could enjoy the changing of the seasons as reflected on the river, the quaint country lane leading to our home and the dense wooded area surrounding it. It was an ideal place for a young family to grow in health, comfort and beauty.

There was only one thing missing... Togetherness! I, the father, could not be there to watch, play and grow with my sons ... or to stroll peacefully with my wife through the vernal splendor that surrounded us. The reason ... the acquiring of the wherewithal that had made this (our first house) possible, had become a time-demanding taskmaster.

I was (and am) an actor. By 1943, my abilities had become much in demand in the flourishing radio broadcasting industry. I was engaged in as many as 35 programs a week ... from soap operas to the top dramatic and comedy shows. Because of the three hour time difference between the East and West coasts, we had to do "repeat broadcasts" for the West. These repeats were done between 11 p.m. and 1 a.m ... so to accomplish my busy schedule, I would leave home about 8:30 in the morning and not return until very late at night. To my sons, a father was someone they saw for a quick moment at breakfast.

Obviously, this was an intolerable situation ... one that could not be resolved without destroying my earning capacity. I had put in many years of hard work as I had grown with the broadcasting industry from its beginnings to the time when Radio was king. TV was then only in the minds of a few pioneers. The obvious answer was to move to the West Coast ... thereby eliminating those home-life destroying repeat broadcasts. BUT — all of my contacts were in New York. The radio industry in Hollywood had its own inner

Alfred Lunt and Alan Reed in *The Pirate*.

circle of actors who did most of the work. I belonged to this select group in New York and knew how hard it was for outsiders to crash the big time.

My long-suffering, lonely wife and I searched for the solution in the wee hours of many mornings. It finally came ... but required very long-range planning. The answer was a motion picture con-tract to assure west coast income while I would be assaulting the pinnacles of West coast radio. But how to accomplish this? I was unknown to the motion picture producers. They only recruited new talent from those who had proven themselves on the Broadway stage. The theatre, then, would have to become my stepping-stone to Hollywood.

This meant giving up about 90% of my radio programs. It was a rough decision. Aside from the monetary loss, it meant closing

Alan Reed in *The Pirate*.

hard-won doors behind me. If I failed in the new approach, it would be very difficult to get back into radio. Producers and directors would not take kindly to one who had let them down ... But, if I wanted a family life (which I did above all else), it had to be done.

I had written contracts with only two programs — *Abie's Irish Rose* and *The Fred Allen Show* — these I had to fulfill. I informed everyone else that I was no longer available, and began making the rounds of the Broadway producers.

I was fortunate. The Theatre Guild was starring Walter Huston in a new [William] Saroyan play, *Love's Old Sweet Song*. A character called "Stylianos Americanos," a Greek-American wrestler, was introduced in the third act. I read for the part and was chosen. The first step had been taken. "Stylianos" was a showy part and I was well received. This play was followed by another for the Theatre Guild — *Hope for a Harvest*, in which I was co-starred with Frederic March and his charming and talented wife, Florence Eldridge. For my performance as an elderly Italian fruit grower, I was nominated for "Best Actor of the Season" by the Broadway Critics Circle.

By this time there were some tentative feelers from Hollywood, but I didn't think I was quite ready. I had to choose between going into motion pictures with a small reputation — or trying to build a larger one, thereby enhancing my chances for a better west coast contract.

I decided to gamble that a building opportunity would present itself. I was lucky — it did — soon after. I was offered the title role in *The Pirate* in support of the foremost acting team in the American theatre — Alfred Lunt and Lynn Fontanne. This was not only a great opportunity to learn, but, because of Lunt's prestige, I would be seen by the heads of all the movie studios. It worked … I was offered contracts by every major producer on the coast.

Now came the need for another major decision. I had arrived at the successful conclusion of my original plan … but now I hesitated. I wasn't sure that signing a long-term contract with one of the major studios would give me the future freedom I wanted. Hume Cronyn, a good friend, was under contract to MGM, and he was very unhappy. They were giving him nothing but bits to play. He had no control over his career for the next seven years. We know, of course, that his studio finally realized that they were wasting a great talent and his career zoomed — but it took a long time. Hume advised me to have my agent find a good one-picture deal. If this could be found, I would control my future. I took his advice. Three weeks went by — my agent had not found a suitable role. He talked of one great possibility, but it was at least a month off.

Meanwhile, MGM had dangled a sizable bit of bait, *if* I would sign a seven-year contract. Their New York executive had promised that I would play "Nero" in their forthcoming production of *Quo Vadis*. This was indeed an inducement. If I could make a hit in a key role in a big production, I'd really be established. So we come to that eventful Friday, April 30, 1943. I had regretfully discarded Hume's advice and told MGM to draw up the contract. This was the signing day.

At the MGM office, I read the contract very carefully throughout. Not one word about "Nero" or *Quo Vadis*. When I questioned this, the executive hemmed and hawed and explained that this was a term contract and had to be separate from a production contract. When I reiterated that the "Nero" role was my only inducement for signing a long-term deal and that the situation could be covered by a separate letter of intent, I was told that he was sure that could be done, but he'd have to take it up with the coast ... but he couldn't very well do that until he sent the signed contract out to them. Now I remembered part of Hume's warning. He had said that all kinds of promises had been made and never fulfilled. So, I said I was sorry, but if they couldn't guarantee the role, I couldn't sign the contract. My talk was much braver than the feelings in the pit of my stomach. And then, that Guardian Angel who has followed me through all the years, showed his hand.

I was waiting for the elevator, after leaving the MGM office, when a secretary came out and said, "Mr. Reed, there's a call for you from the coast." It was my agent. He had tracked me down at MGM to tell me that the producer of the independent film that we had talked about had seen me in *The Pirate* and was willing to offer a contract long in advance of production if I could join another actor and come to California the following Monday. *The Pirate* was closing the next night as was another show called *Sons and Soldiers*. The "other actor" was an unknown young man who had made a strong impression in that show. His name was Gregory Peck. I okayed the deal and Greg and I were on our way to our first motion picture.

The only difference was that Greg was signed for eight future pictures and I was signed only for the one I wanted.

I don't know to this day whether it was a right or wrong decision, for I found while making that first picture that an entirely different technique was required for this new medium, and that there was no time to learn it while shooting. At any rate, the picture laid a big egg, and I bombed out completely. Had I taken the long-term contract, the studio, having an investment in me, might have brought me along slowly until I was ready to impress. As it turned out, the failure of my first picture caused another major decision.

But that's another story.

"Another story" was not written, but Alan did lay down a taste of what might have been.

CHAPTER 6

Vaudeville

There are two kinds of vaudeville — the old and the new. I participated in both. The reader will be shown that the emerging radio personalities have become the vaudeville headliners of the new. While the old vaudeville existed long before radio, it was thought advisable to put this chapter after the chapter on Radio because most of my vaudeville appearances occurred after I became known through radio. The chapter will also show my unexpected debut into the old. It usually takes about 10 years of hard work playing what was known as "the small time" before an act or performer could even hope to aspire to the "Big Time" of the Keith-Albee circuit. With me it was the opposite. Through a "once in a lifetime" opportunity I broke in at the pinnacle of all vaudeville houses — The Palace in New York!

This chapter will include many anecdotes about the old vaudeville and also the new. It will show the rise of the "Presentation Houses" — elaborate stage productions in support of the movies which were now the true headliners. Also included will be exclusive tales of my association with Bob Hope and of my partnership with Bert Gordon, "the Mad Russian." There will be much humor in this chapter.

As Sir Toby Belch in *Twelfth Night*

CHAPTER 7

Legitimate Broadway Theater

With my new name I am now pursuing a planned course, the objective of which is a motion picture contract. In order to accomplish this, good roles must be found on the Broadway stage. I did five plays in all: *A House in the Country* (seven performances), and *Double Dummy* (approximately four weeks).

After these two flops I became a Theatre Guild actor. I appeared in three plays for them before going to Hollywood: *Love's Old Sweet Song* by William Saroyan and starring Walter Huston. (This chapter will dwell at length on my close friendship with Walter.) It started with this play which ran about ten weeks including four weeks of break-ins out of town.

Next came *Hope for a Harvest* (picked as one of the ten best plays by Burns Mantle). This play starred Frederic March and his wife Florence Eldridge; I was featured in a most colorful part — a part that generated critical acclaim and won me a nomination as Best Actor of the season by the New York Drama Critic's Circle.

This was followed by my most rewarding experience — the title role in S.N. Behrman's *The Pirate*, starring Alfred Lunt and Lynn Fontanne.

This chapter will include many humorous and human anecdotes of my experiences with the greats of the Broadway theatre. It will be treated with the love and respect I hold the Legitimate Theatre to this day.

It will also dwell on a most unusual production of Shakespeare's *Twelfth Night* by Huntington Hartford and my first starring role in the Theatre Guild production of *The Merry Wives of Windsor*, in which I replaced Charles Coburn.

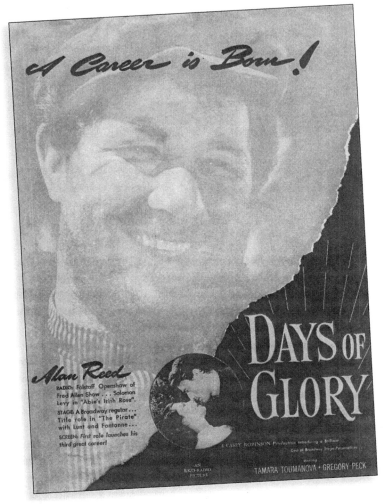

It is interesting that Alan decided to take his wife's father's middle name as his own last name, but a shame he didn't spend more time describing his "long-suffering wife." Alan Reed, Jr. takes up the task below:

"My mother Finette Walker Reed was born on June 10, 1909 in Lake Linden, Michigan, to Vitaline Pijean, a pioneer type of French Canadian stock, and Myron Walker, a mining engineer from Washington, DC. At about ten years of age she and her younger brother Robert (Uncle Bud) moved with their parents to Peru where Myron led a mining company in Cerro de Pasco, high above Lima. Mom's younger sister Margaret (Aunt Peggy) was born there. The family stayed there for two or three years.

"Returning to Washington, Finette continued her schooling, enjoying playing piano and singing along the way. She attended George Washington University

and in her early twenties managed to fulfill a dream—moving to New York to pursue a musical career. She shared an apartment with a girlfriend and did secretarial work while auditioning for shows. With luck and perseverance (not to mention her lovely voice, tall, thin figure and pretty face) she worked in the chorus of a number of Broadway shows, including Show Boat, Music in the Air, and Anything Goes, the latter starring Ethel Merman. Her fellow chorus member in that show was Vivian Vance, later of I Love Lucy fame.

"One little job she got in 1933 resulted in the golden opportunity of a lifetime. She had been hired by CBS as a model to sit in a studio in front of some lights and a camera wearing a sort of green makeup. The radio network was experimenting with the new technology of television. As it happened, a radio actor named Teddy Bergman was walking in the hallway and, peering through the glass in the door to the studio, saw the attractive but oddly-hued lady. Waiting for her to finish, he asked her for coffee in the lobby diner, and the two struck up a relationship. They were married in April, 1934. Mom never returned to the stage but continued to practice her piano and sing at parties and gatherings.

"The Reed family, now with three sons, moved to Beverly Hills in 1943. Dad had been working on his first Hollywood movie that summer (Days of Glory, starring Gregory Peck, was also the first movie for Peck and much of the cast) so it was up to Mom to gather her boys, vacate the house in Riverdale, and board the train for California. The last stop of the three-day trip was Pasadena, and Mom was readying herself and the boys for arrival in Los Angeles when a porter came to the door and said there was a visitor. We were silent as a large man with a full beard walked in. The first sound heard was from Kit, the youngest — "Daddy!" And, of course, it was. He wanted to surprise us and arrive together with us. And maybe show off the beard he grew for the movie.

"Finette had been active in local community affairs in New York and continued that involvement in California. PTA and the Cub Scouts were of special interest to her. In the 1960s she studied and attained a real estate license and became affiliated with a leading realty company in Beverly Hills, where she represented the sale of numerous houses to friends and others. Later, she would assist Dad regularly in his specialty advertising business, Alan Reed Enterprises.

"All through her life Finette had an inquisitive mind. Her mother was a devout Catholic and so was she. She was raised with discipline and a sense of order and had an appreciation, without pretension, of the finer things. She spoke Spanish and had a great interest in the English language, its roots and proper usage. A certain elegance and refinement were a part of her aura. One of her most joyous occasions was the celebration in 1999 of her 90th birthday. A large gathering at a restaurant in Malibu brought friends and relations from all over to celebrate with her. Nothing pleased her more than to walk gracefully among the tables and be surrounded once more by all the important people in her life.

"Her eyesight had grown to virtually nil, and by 2003 her general health had declined to where she rarely left the house. With the help of a loving caregiver she *continued to get up each day, listen to her Braille books on tape, follow the news on television, hear with great interest about her sons' and their families' lives, and even practice her piano playing.*

"On October 15, 2005, at age 96, Finette passed away in a most peaceful manner, having knelt in prayer and now asleep in her bed."

Finette and the kids, circa 2000 (posing as in the earlier photo on page 70).

CHAPTER 8

Motion Pictures

It was thought that the events leading up to my departure for the west coast would do better to begin this chapter. Hence the revision of what had been a first-person presentation is included. We continue now after shooting has begun on *Days of Glory*, the first picture.

The switch to the new medium was disastrous from the word go! After seven weeks of shooting, the picture was closed down for four days, because the front office at RKO didn't like what was coming up in the daily rushes. After the four-day layoff, $800,000 was cut from the budget, and out the window went my best scenes, including a heroic death scene which really made the part. The events leading up to this will be fleshed out, and should give the reader an intimate look into the many vagaries that can influence the motion picture product before it reaches the public.

During this first picture I will learn that (unless one is a star with draw capacity) the actor is just a puppet to be moved about at will. From then on, my only reason to make a movie would be the excellent script involved. I hated the confines of the medium.

Again, the author reminds you that everything accounted herein takes place during an ongoing radio career. In all I appeared in approximately 50 motion pictures, including *Nob Hill*, *The Postman Always Rings Twice*, *I, the Jury*, *Desperate Hours*, *Actors and Sin*, *Ladies of the Jury*, *Emergency Wedding*, *The Redhead and the Cowboy*, *Breakfast at Tiffany's*, *Dream of Kings*, and in 1977, *The Seniors* (a current picture, not yet released).

The Seniors, incidentally, provided the first time I felt creative in a movie. It was my most pleasant motion picture experience. There will be tales and anecdotes connected with each picture, which will make the chapter both amusing and informative.

Alan was usually relegated to "supporting player" status in films, though some of his roles were indeed pivotal and showed off his flair for larger-than-life characters. He virtually eclipsed Marlon Brando in their brief scenes together in *Viva Zapata!* (1952). Portraying real-life Mexican patriot, General Pancho Villa, he didn't appear until more than halfway through the film. Still, his two scenes were both with Brando, and Alan's grandiose, booming voice portrayal easily overshadowed the phlegmatic star.

Cast party for *Days of Glory,* 1944. Gregory Peck is in the center.

Alan Reed, Jr. recalled, "His main scene in that was with Marlon Brando, each of them lying under the shade of a tree, Villa recalling earlier days. It was shot on the back lot of 20th Century-Fox (now Century City) and I remember Dad telling us how the director, Elia Kazan, helped him prepare for the scene. He lay down on top of him and, quietly in his ear, asked him to think about Teddy Bergman back in New York in the early days of radio and the hectic, thrilling pace of going from one show to another across the hall or across town. That sense memory suggestion must have helped; it was a good scene, ending with Villa turning to Zapata urging him, 'you be president.'

"One other thing I remember about Dad's experience in that film. He had blue eyes, and Pancho Villa, a Mexican, had brown eyes. Contact lenses in 1952 were not as small or so easily worn as today. He was fitted with brown lenses, and it took quite a while to get used to them before filming."

Viva Zapata!, written by legendary novelist John Steinbeck, was nominated for several Oscars, winning Best Supporting Actor for Anthony Quinn's brilliant portrayal of Zapata's faithful, and later disillusioned, brother Eufemio.

Reed's best-remembered film role was that of good-natured blackmailer, Ezra Kennedy, in *The Postman Always Rings Twice* (1946). Most of the film takes place at a roadside restaurant owned and operated by elderly Nick Smith (Cecil Kellaway). After the very young and beautiful Cora Smith (Lana Turner) and drifter Frank Chambers (John Garfield) successfully kill Cora's husband, the two are almost convicted of murder. Luckily, she's hired

the very clever attorney Arthur Keats (Hume Cronyn) to look out for her. District Attorney Kyle Sackett (Leon Ames) manipulates Frank into such an emotional state that he signs a confession claiming that Cora alone had carried out the murder.

Cora becomes so livid she can't *wait* to dictate the truth to the DA. In comes Ezra to type up her complete statement; but he's followed by Keats who admits that Ezra doesn't work for the DA; he simply works for him, as his own private dick. Explaining to the heated couple that it was for her own good, it seems it was better for her to get the "truth" out of her system rather than blab to the DA. The maneuver works, and Cora is acquitted via probation, while the State isn't interested in Frank at all. Because of all this, there's a lengthy estrangement between the lovers.

That is, until Ezra steps back in the picture.

He's had a falling out with his boss, and is eager to collect some blackmail money — say about $15k — before skipping out of town. The couple pretends to go along with the scheme, especially with Ezra holding a gun on them, but Frank is quick to splash a drink in the big guy's face and rough him up. Under duress, the private dick agrees to call his friend who is holding the transcribed confession. Ezra endures several blows to the face before he's thrown out of the house, yet still has enough compassion (or stupidity) to utter "Gesundheit" when Frank sneezes.

Alan Reed, Jr. recalled, *"My wife reminded me of a story I had told her about Dad's poker club. Every Monday night he had a group of guys, including some movie business luminaries, over to the house to play poker. Among the players were Lee J.*

Cobb, John Garfield, and Joseph Gershenson, head of music production at Universal Studios. My grandmother Vital (Finette's mom) was living with us and was given the job of setting up and serving snacks and goodies to the guys, usually around midnight. She would buy all the deli items and pastries and have it ready for them, paying for them out of the pot where all the winnings went. She loved doing this.

"*Once, during the time Dad was filming* The Postman Always Rings Twice *at MGM, a funny thing happened. A scene in the film culminated in a fight between Garfield's character and Dad's where Dad is either pinned down or up against a wall and Garfield has to slap him hard several times across the face. Garfield felt some trepidation about doing this, but Dad said go ahead, don't worry, do it. Maybe sensing a little embarrassment afterwards, Dad decided to play around with him that night at the poker game. He called the others and had them come a little early with some alternate apparel. When Garfield arrived, he found the poker club had become a sewing circle with a group of nice little ladies sitting around. I don't recall hearing his reaction, but hopefully they all enjoyed a good laugh. And regarding that pot where all the winnings went: At Christmas each year it was donated to one of two charities — the Vista Del Mar Home in West Los Angeles or the Little Flower Home for Children. I think those Monday evenings went on for at least five years.*"

Alan did indeed love his card games. As one of his grandchildren (Tony Reed) recalled: "At Alan and Finette's Queen's Road home, they had a lower level beneath the main living area of the home. It wasn't quite a 'downstairs' area, but rather an area which had to be accessed separately from outside the house — almost like an attached guesthouse. As little children, we grandkids loved to go in that section of the house. To me, it always seemed like we were sneaking away to this special place away from the adults.

"The centerpiece of this area was a large poker table in the middle of the main room. Teddy loved to play cards, and so did [we], although I'm not so sure how keen he was on the idea of us using his beautiful table for our entertainment.

"It was at this table that he taught me a critical life lesson that was burned into my being from that moment on. My brother Alex and I were playing with a deck of cards that Grandpa Teddy [Alan] used in his poker games. Teddy came in and glanced over at us. At that moment, I happened to be bending the edge of one of my cards in a playful way. Well, as any card player can tell you, altering the form of just a single card renders the entire deck damaged and useless.

"Upon seeing my handy work, Teddy's bellowing voice rained down over me like I had never heard. He was understandably upset that I had ruined one of his special decks of cards, and he proceeded to teach me the lesson about why you simply can't do that to playing cards.

"That moment has never left me, and to this day, I look for the opportunity to admonish children everywhere about keeping a deck of cards pure and without imperfections!"

One of Alan's most unusual films, *Actors and Sin* (1952), was divided into two parts. The first half ("Actor's Blood") starred Edward G. Robinson as the father of a troubled child actress; Alan took on the role of J.B. Cobb in the "Woman of Sin" second half, concerning the improbable life of a nine-year-old romance writer.

Alan Reed, Jr. again recalled, *"Dad took me to the set one day and showed me what they were getting ready to shoot. It was a long series of large office doors,*

Actors & Sin, 1952.

each one opening to the next — all leading to the biggest one of all for the office of the head of the movie studio, played by guess who. His character was constantly being frustrated by the demands of the little girl.

"This was a small film with a small release. I thought Dad was great in it. He made me laugh. This role led to his being cast as J.B. Hafter, head of the studio in the short-lived TV series Mr. Adams and Eve *starring Howard Duff and Ida Lupino, who were married in real life. On the show they played movie stars married to each other and who cause continual grief and aggravation to the studio head who is always trying to placate them."* [The series produced 66 episodes filmed over a two-year period; it was nominated for three Emmys.]

At this point in his career, Alan Reed was working in all forms of media.

He returned briefly to radio in Stan Freberg's first major radio series, *That's Rich*, which had its audition show on November 12, 1953 and ran on Friday nights from January 8 to May 21, 1954, then on Thursday nights at 9 from July 15 to September 23, 1954.

One of Reed's best villainous film parts came in 1955 as he tried to foil the Lewis & Clark expedition in *The Far Horizons.* As the famed explorers enter Indian territory, William Clark (Charlton Heston) begins to slowly fall for the lovely Indian maiden, Sacagawea (Donna Reed), and vice versa. Little does anyone know that the chief of the people who captured her and who treat her as a slave has promised French trader Charbonneau (Alan Reed) that he could

The Far Horizons, 1955.

have her, in exchange for leading the US military troops the wrong way and helping to stage a surprise attack against them. Luckily his mutiny is foiled and the Indians are resisted, but Charboneau's failure depresses him, causing him to drink to excess. The night ends in a fight between himself and Clark that is almost a tie. Clark gets the better of him and sends the disgusted Frenchman on his way home with enough food and water to get him out of there.

Nineteen fifty-five was also the year he opened Alan Reed Enterprises which supplied and distributed a Reedline brand of cigarette lighters. Coincidentally, Mel Blanc started his own business — an advertising agency — around the time he was working with Alan on *The Flinstones*. In

Showing off the Flower Pen to the public.

1961 Alan sold the distributor side of the business and opened up a branch office in Franklin Square, New York, so he could concentrate solely on supplying the product. For "most intriguing new product" the Advertising Specialty Guild International presented Alan with an Award of Merit at their annual show. This was for the "flower pen" which sported a few leaves, a flowerpot desktop holder and an artificial bloom in order to give the customer "a touch of spring at her fingertips — the 'just right' goodwill-builder designed to please the fair sex." Unfortunately, as most successful items are, it was copied by several competitors and offered at a lower price.

In 1965 Alan's youngest son Chris ("Kit") Reed joined him in the business, and after taking a couple of years to learn the trade, took it over in 1967. Alan officially retired from the business then, but he and his wife continued to come in regularly. Kit changed the name of the company to Reed Enterprises, which eventually grew to a sales force of over 50 people. In 1985 he again changed the company name to "Logomotion." He operates the business out of his home to the present day.

Marjorie Morningstar, a 1958 film based on Herman Wouk's novel, starred Gene Kelly and Natalie Wood and featured Alan Reed in a small but colorful

role. He plays a low comic in need of an onstage assistant. In his crumpled hat and red-striped shirt (complete with oversized white boutonnière), he flirts outrageously with the title character, a would-be actress, during a spirited audition.

It is unfortunate that Alan was so underused in his biggest film, *Breakfast at Tiffany's* (1961). While his character was an important piece of the two-hour romance, Alan as Sally Tomato has only a brief scene as the narcotics mobster whom Audrey Hepburn (as Holly Golightly) visits for the sum of $100 weekly. She innocently passes on to him the "weather report," a coded message that gives the crook an idea of how his illicit business is going. She takes weather reports back as well, such as "Snow flurries expected this weekend in New Orleans," as he tells her upon leaving Sing-Sing. Near the film's end, she's arrested (for unwittingly helping Sally) and then released on bail. She visits him once more, off-camera, during the film, but sadly for Alan, it wasn't a part of the finished film. This is odd, considering how large a set was used for the brief jail visit. Regardless of his limited screen time, Alan called *Breakfast at Tiffany's* his favorite film role and spoke of it with fondness.

CHAPTER 9

Television

My overlapping career included regular appearances on television from 1947 to 1967. As radio began its fadeout and TV its rise, I found myself in a strange position. Through the radio years I enjoyed a very large income due to the *many* jobs I did each week. However, I could not promote my name because the programs I was on were in many cases sponsored by direct competitors. My characters appeared on shows for three insurance companies, four cereal accounts, and two cigarette manufacturers, etc. So that if the name Alan Reed was pushed on any one show, the other competitive sponsors would holler: "Get that guy off our show...he's on for the opposition!"

The result being that, with the advent of television, I found myself with not enough "Name" to warrant my own show, and had to be satisfied with being a "second banana." In radio this was alright because of the multiple jobs, but in TV one could do only one show a week, thereby providing much less income than that provided in radio. So, having taken on many financial responsibilities, I had to augment my income.

For the second time in my career, I started a business — Alan Reed Enterprises — Specialty: Advertising. (Will be explained at length.)

It is the author's wish that the blacklisting mentioned in the chapter on radio be moved to this chapter. This chapter will also include the story of Tim and Irene Ryan ... how Tim couldn't make the transition and how Irene went on to become the much loved "Granny" on *The Beverly Hillbillies.*

From Chuck Schaden's interview:

You said you were on the TV version of Luigi. *Did you make a fairly easy transition from radio to television?*

Well, yes, and I had done some TV before that, but it wasn't the kind of transition that I wanted. I'll tell you why. I had spent most of my time in radio doing an average of thirty-five programs a week. The money was very good, and with money you acquire responsibilities. Coming into television, you can only do one, at most two programs a week. I hadn't built enough of a name to be the star of a show where the money would be comparable. So, I decided that I'd better have something else going because I had a big home and family to support. Schools and things like that. I started a business in specialty advertising. This was twenty years ago. My son is running the business today. It was quite successful and my younger son has made it even more so. I've retired.

From that business, but not from show biz?

Well, the only thing I do is Flintstones or Flintstone-connected things now, and that is commercials. I do have a major activity now that I'm very excited about. I'm on the Board of Directors and Finance Chairman of a group called Theatre Forty. We're sponsored by the city of Beverly Hills. Beverly Hills is the only high school in the country that has, in residence, our own theater, which was built for us.

CHAPTER 10

Off Camera
or Voice Over

This will deal mainly with what a radio actor is trained for. The term is "off camera" or "voice over." It is what one hears daily on commercials and scripts which are animated cartoons. Participation in this remunerative field is what has occupied me for the past 18 years.

This chapter will contain an unexpected, in-depth conversation with the greatest genius of animated cartoons…Walt Disney. It will also include the beginnings of the Hanna-Barbera studio and the rise of *The Flintstones* to its present point of becoming a standard. I am and have been for 18 years the voice of Fred Flintstone! It is happy work for me, which takes me back to my first love — radio. It has also been a blessing which has confirmed my belief in a Master Plan. For the past ten years of my life I have seen many and varied assaults on my health. Physically I would not have been able to work in any of the other related fields of show business. So I constantly thank The Lord and Hanna-Barbera.

This chapter will also relate the coining of the catchphrase, "Yabba Dabba Doo" and near the end, we'll hear me use this phrase to denote much happiness, as I sit with my wife, my three sons and their wives and my ten grandchildren, celebrating Finette's and my 45th wedding anniversary. I will also summarize my 56 years in show business.

The Flintstones has been an icon of American television for nearly 50 years and should require no explanation here. But for those readers living in caves (or under a rock), it was a cartoon version of Jackie Gleason's *The Honeymooners* — only set during the Stone Age. Ralph and Alice Kramdem essentially became Fred and Wilma Flintstone (Alan Reed and Jean Vander Pyle) and Ed and Trixie Norton became Barney and Betty Rubble (Mel Blanc and Bea Benaderet). The half-hour animated series was immensely popular with children and adults alike and was seen in primetime on the ABC television network from its debut in 1960 to its cancellation in 1966. It went on to play in syndication for decades.

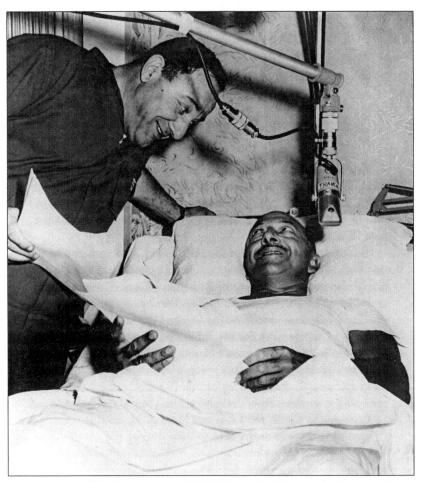

Alan recording *The Flintstones* with Mel Blanc after his near-fatal car accident.

Co-creator Joe Barbera auditioned a multitude of actors for the voices of the four Flintstone (then still named *The Flagstones*) main characters. One of the aspiring "Freds" was Bill Thompson, famous as "Droopy" in cartoons and a variety of characters on the *Fibber McGee & Molly* radio show. It seemed that Bill couldn't sustain the "gravelly" quality for the length of time that Joe needed, so they had to look elsewhere.

Old Hanna-Barbera stalwart Daws Butler tested for voices of both Fred and Barney, but Joe wasn't happy with how the vocal qualities were matching up with his take on the personalities. Though five shows were already recorded, Barbera brought in seasoned radio veterans Mel Blanc and Alan Reed to read for the parts, and that's all it took. Barbera closed his eyes and heard the humor and warmth in Fred's voice, even during Mr. Flintstone's particularly grouchy moments.

Jean "Wilma Flintstone" Vander Pyl said, "That was Alan. He played sort of an exaggerated side of himself. He was a very warm human being. He had such a childlike charm with a very high respect for women, and he just loved children. He could laugh at himself and then sometimes get real fatherly and talk to you in that [concerned] tone."

The only trouble with identifying so closely to a character was that Alan wasn't allowed to provide many incidental or supporting characters, as Mel Blanc did throughout the series. There were a few miscellaneous characters he played along the show's run, but Fred's rock-head personality was so much larger than life, and the show so popular, it would overshadow the rest of his career. He would forever be Fred.

There was even a Flintstones film in 1966. *The Man Called Flintstone* was the only feature film released during the original cartoon's heyday, and still holds up as well as the television shows. The often subtle blend of James Bond/*Maltese Falcon* spoofing and Stone Age invention combine at a different pace from the half-hour series, but a generous helping of songs from John McCarthy and Doug Goodwin give it almost the same campy quality as an *Our Man Flint* from the same era. The voice pool was the same as the series, (minus Bea Benaderet, who would die two years later), and boasted an amazing supporting cast, including June Foray, Paul Frees and Daws Butler.

In the film, Fred Flintstone just happens to be a dead ringer for master spy Rock Slag (Paul Frees), who was put out of commission by an evil henchmen of the sinister Green Goose (Harvey Korman), head of SMIRK (the Stone Age Secret Service). Fred's assignment: to impersonate Rock and track down the Green Goose and his seductive accomplice, Tanya (June Foray). Fred and Barney and the families head for Paris, then Rome, to grab hold of Tanya, who soon leads Fred and Barney into a trap. They end up as prisoners in an abandoned amusement park, which is really the Green Goose's secret headquarters. The boys just manage to resist the GG's torture until the real Rock Slag arrives to thwart the evildoer's ambitious plan to conquer all of Eu-rock. Once the madman is captured, he and his co-conspirators, including Tanya, are tricked into their own secret missile and shot into outer space. With Eu-rock saved, Fred and the clan wearily — but happily — return to Bedrock.

Alan Reed, Jr. recalled, *"All I remember about* The Man Called Flintstone *was that it was very exciting at the time, seeing a big screen version of the TV show with the expanded production values. Dad was very happy about it."*

The Flintstones, still going strong in camp grounds across the country!
PHOTO COURTESY OF FLINTSTONES BEDROCK CITY, CUSTER, SD.

Henry Corden doubled as Fred's singing voice both on the series and in the feature film. (Corden ultimately took over as the character's speaking voice after Alan's death.) As Jean Vander Pyl admitted, "Alan could sing, but not in the right key. Henry could do great harmonies when it was called for and gave a competent F. Flintstone impression, though Alan Reed *owned* Fred Flintstone. No one was a threat to that inspired merging between gentle actor and loud-mouthed caveman."

As Alan told Chuck Schaden:

Let's talk about The Flintstones. *When did that first come along?*

Nineteen-sixty; this is our 15th year.

And you're still doing new programs?

No, no, no. There is a new program being offered. It hasn't been sold yet. It would be great if they could sell it, but so far they haven't been able to. It's called "The Flintstones Fuzz," in which Barney and I would be policemen. Cops. It would be a satire on the police shows that are all around.

How many of those shows did you make altogether?

One hundred sixty-six of the original *Flintstones* and 26 of *Pebbles and Bam Bam* in which each of the Flintstones have segments and the kids have segments. But they're repeated and repeated and repeated. My residuals ran out long ago, but what's great about it is the commercials. I have between eight and sixteen commercials going every year for Flintstones products [Fruity Pebbles cereal, Flintstones Vitamins, etc.]. They keep running them and playing them.

Well, that's good. You were working with Mel Blanc on that show.

Mel and I worked together very closely.

Fred became part of Alan; and vice versa. He would make personal appearances in his own leopard-skin costume, caveman-black wig, and bare legs. He loved kids and would often wish the little ones "a special Yabba-Dabba-Doo to you!" on their birthdays.

His grandson Tony recalled one such incident. "One day at Carpenter Avenue Elementary, I was fortunate enough to bring my actual grandfather to Show & Tell day in our class. I was in third grade, so this was in the early

Hoagy Carmichael and Alan Reed at a *Flintstones* recording session.

'70s. I waited for him to arrive just outside my classroom, my heart beating fast in anticipation of his arrival.

"When we stepped into the class together, there was a buzz of excitement. I doubt anyone had even seen a cartoon character in the flesh before! He was very gracious with his time, explaining to everyone about how he became the voice of Fred. He gave a sampling of his various cartoon voices, then, finally, belted out a 'Yabba Dabba Doo!' Needless to say, I was quite a popular guy in class that day. It still brings a smile to my face."

Alan Reed Jr. summed up his father best when he said, *"Words that come to mind when I think of people's first impression when meeting him are 'warm,' 'friendly,' 'earnest,' and 'cute.' He had a welcoming personality and a generous nature, which became quite evident on getting to know him. A devout believer in the equality of man, he was passionate against any sign of injustice, individual or societal."*

CHAPTER 11

Yabba Dabba Doo!

Alan Reed, Jr. stated, *"For me, the biggest link between Dad and Fred was his hearty chuckle and the twinkle in his eyes, which you could almost hear in his voice. The sometimes gruff, blowhard aspects of Fred were usually evident in Dad only when telling a joke or fooling around."*

When Alan wrote an article entitled, "Yabba Dabba Doo!" he dedicated it to Dr. J.J. Kaufman, Chief of the Urological Department, Professor of Surgery in Urology at the UCLA Medical Center in Westwood, California.

"YABBA DABBA DOO!" exclaimed the young intern. "It's working!"

Hearing those three words of gobbledegook may have saved my life.

It was January 24th, 1970 and I was in the Intensive Care Unit of UCLA's magnificent hospital in Westwood, California. It was the morning of my third day in Intensive Care. I was still in that drug-induced torpor that usually follows a major operation. I was despondent to the point of not caring whether I lived or died. For two days of wild hallucination combined with what I thought was lucid conversation with my wife, my three sons and my doctor, my subconscious had picked up the feeling that the operation was a failure. That I was doomed. I thought I had heard my doctor, the renowned J.J. Kaufman, Chief of Urology at UCLA say, "I can't understand why it isn't working." Later I found that he had, in fact, used those words. I wasn't sure what he meant, but it plunged me into the depths of despair.

And then, on that third morning, hearing that "YABBA DABBA DOO!"—everything changed. As the words cut through my semi-comatose despondency, I smiled and perked up immediately. I just *knew* everything was going to be all right.

For those three crazy, double-talk words were of my creation…
and hearing them used naturally, to express delight, in these somber
surroundings was the tonic that brought me out of my despair.

Here's how it all began.

My three little words were born in 1960. Bill Hanna and Joe
Barbera were planning a new cartoon series for television. It was

to be called *The Flintstones*. I was chosen to be the voice of Fred
Flintstone.

At the outset I realized that here was an opportunity to promote
what is known as a "catch-phrase" in the world of show business.
In the early days of radio, the airwaves were full of them. Jack
Pearl had "Vas you dere, Sharlie?" — Joe Penner his "Wanna buy
a duck?" etc. I brought this thought to Joe Barbera, who produced
and directed The Flintstones. When he agreed, I volunteered to
find the right words.

Inasmuch as "Fred" was an exuberant character, I thought I'd
try to find a phrase that could be used to express excitement or
glee. I started with the first word that popped into my mind …

the old cowboy expression, "YAHOO!" For the next few days my wife must have thought I'd gone off my rocker, as I went around the house uttering the strangest sounds like: "Yahoodeldoodle," "Doodle de dough-dough," "Dabble-de doo-roo," finally I hit on "Yabba Doo" and I felt I was close…but it needed a little something more. I added the middle "Dabba" and my brain-child was born… "YABBA DABBA DOO!"

Little did I know that those three weird sounds would have such a profound influence on my life!

Now…eleven years later, *The Flintstones* has become a standard TV attraction and "YABBA DABBA DOO!" a commonly used phrase to express enthusiasm. Of course, I don't take too seriously the fact that these silly words of mine have become part of our language, but I must admit that I got the thrill of my life when I heard Astronaut Wally Shirra use them on a telecast seen and heard by millions of people all over the world!

It was October 11, 1968, and Apollo VII was testing the new Spacecraft Propulsion System. This was the system that eventually was used to begin the second stage of our moon flights. It was the first time it was being tested with astronauts riding the capsule. The test was made about 110 miles up from Earth in Zero Gravity. As always, there was close contact between NASA headquarters in Houston and the spaceship. About 2½ hours after blastoff another countdown was in order before the Spacecraft Propulsion System was to be fired…10…9…8…7…6…5…4…3…2…1… AND AWAY IT WENT! Seconds later, the voice of Wally Shirra was heard all over the world shouting: "TESTED!"… "LIKE A BOMB!"… "YABBA DABBA DOO!"… "WHAT A RIDE!" My answering yell must have been heard all the way back to the Space Capsule.

After that, during the making of each new *Flintstone* episode, I experienced a new feeling of pride every time I said, "Yabba Dabba Doo!"

And then the blow struck! What began as a routine physical examination ended with the dreaded word…CANCER! After describing a bleeding symptom to my doctor, he immediately ordered X-rays of my bladder. When the pictures were developed, he showed me an X-ray picture of a normal bladder and pointed out the overall whiteness of it. On my picture about half of the bladder was spotted and darker. This meant tumors. He would have to cystoscope me and take a biopsy to see if the tumors were benign or malignant. Two days later he operated to remove the cancerous tumors from my bladder.

My recovery was quick. The doctor was sure that he had been able to remove everything. "But," he explained, "to be on the safe side, you'd better have a cystoscopic checkup in about two months."

I had been feeling fine, and when I again checked into the hospital I felt it was just for a routine precautionary measure (which it was), but it ended in a nosedive for my soaring spirits. The insidious invader had come back twofold. The tumors were racing upward toward my kidneys. The only way to prevent this surely fatal incursion was to remove the bladder, the urethra and the prostate gland. This was a six-hour operation and one which my doctor, a much-respected urologist, felt himself too old to attempt. He suggested that two men had had remarkable success with this most difficult operation: Dr. Kaufman, at UCLA, and Dr. Govan, at Stanford University. He emphasized the need for haste if the tumors were to be prevented from reaching the kidneys. My home being in Los Angeles, I called UCLA.

"Dr. Kaufman's office," the impersonal voice announced.

"I have to have an emergency appointment with Dr. Kaufman," I said, identifying myself.

"I'm sorry, Mr. Reed, but Dr. Kaufman is in Europe. He's not due back until November 21st."

That was two weeks away. In desperation, I made an appointment to see him then.

Wanting a corroborating opinion, I called Dr. Govan at Stanford. He very graciously agreed to see me the next morning and I flew up to Palo Alto.

After still another cystoscopic examination, Dr. Govan informed me that the operation was not only necessary, but that if we were to win the race for my kidneys, it should be done within ten days.

"Doctor," I said, "I read an article that told of much success in treating cancer by the use of cobalt, can't we try that?"

"Mr. Reed," he replied, "I had the chief of radiology with me when I examined you. We hoped it would be possible to give you the cobalt treatment, but unfortunately there are inaccessible areas, the bladder will have to come out. Don't wait."

I wanted the operation to be done at UCLA, near my home and family. This meant that if the ten-day deadline was to be met, Dr. Kaufman would have to operate on me immediately after our first talk. Dr. Govan sent a four-page letter outlining his findings. It was on Dr. Kaufman's desk when I arrived for my November 21st appointment.

Dr. Kaufman impressed me immediately. His manner, his keen-ness of eye, his relaxed, confidence-inspiring composure assured me that his great international reputation was not unfounded.

"Doctor," I said, after we had discussed Dr. Govan's analysis of my case, "I hope you can do this operation immediately…my ten days are up the day after tomorrow."

He looked at me smilingly and replied, "We'll do what we have to do. I'll check you into the hospital this afternoon and I'll cysto-scope you tomorrow morning."

"Not another cystoscope! I've had two of them in the past three weeks. I'm resigned to the fact that the bladder has to come out. Can't you do it tomorrow?"

I have always been the kind of person who, when facing a real-ity, does what is necessary to meet it intelligently. I had pondered my situation from every angle and was now anxious to have the inevitable over and done with.

"Mr. Reed," Dr. Kaufman said calmly, "I have to see your inside situation for myself. Much as I respect the other doctors involved, my decision must be made by my observations. We'll cystoscope you tomorrow morning."

So I checked into UCLA at 4 p.m., and at 7:30 the next morning, Dr. Kaufman got a tube-eye view of my not so lovely interior.

He and my family were waiting when I came out of the mild anesthetic used for a cystoscopy. Everybody was smiling.

"What's everybody so happy about?" I asked, semi-groggily.

"Honey, you don't have to have the operation right away!" my wife blurted out…tears behind her smile.

"Isn't that great, pop?" my three sons echoed.

You can bet that this announcement removed the last vestige of the anesthetic. "What are you talking about? How can that be?" I shrieked.

Dr. Kaufman took over. "Alan," he said, "I've been quite successful with a combination of cobalt radiation and a chemical called 5FU. We're going to try that for a couple of months."

My face fell and the doctor noticed it immediately.

"What's bothering you?"

"Doctor," I replied as I fought for control, "I have thoroughly believed that I had ten days and ten days only before my kidneys would become cancerous. Now you tell me that you're going to try, for a couple of months, a treatment that the top men in Urology and Radiation at Stanford have said could not work."

Dr. Kaufman smiled, and I must admit his warm smile cut right through my agitation. I was able to listen calmly as he said, "Alan, I can't guarantee that this treatment will work for you. I've had some successes and some failures. The medication part of the treatment is relatively new, but I can guarantee that I can slow the advance of the malignancy long enough to give this a try. I'll watch you very closely during this testing period and I promise, at the slightest sign of advance, I'll operate and remove the bladder. Now I want you to understand completely that it's highly possible that the Stanford diagnosis is absolutely correct. But even with only an outside chance, I think it's worth taking the gamble."

Well, of course it was. I had learned by then the mechanics of the operation. The bladder, urethra and prostate gland would be completely removed and I would be provided with a "STOMA." The "stoma" is a small blob of, what appears to be, raw flesh (but is in no way sensitive or painful). Actually, it is the surface area of a conduit to which the "ureters" are connected (ureters are the tubes that pass fluid from the kidneys to the bladder). This conduit is isolated from the main stream of the small intestine. The ureters, which used to pour fluids into the bladder, now pass them into the conduit, which, in turn, eliminates them through the stoma, in which an opening has been made. The stoma protrudes about a half inch from the skin surface. The flow of urine is in no way disturbed. Instead of flowing into the bladder, it goes into a plastic bag that is attached to the skin over the stoma.

Naturally, if there was any way to avoid carrying this "external bladder" I was for it. So, I became an outpatient and the treatments began. Five times a week, specially marked portions of my lower regions were bombarded by UCLA's Linear Accelerator and a Cobalt Unit. This, along with injections of the chemical 5FU. Both of these amazing units have the capacity of emitting rays which penetrate deeply and which can target on the pinpointed, diseased organ, while sparing all other vital organs.

There were no serious ill effects from these treatments, although I must admit my nether regions constantly felt as if they'd been exposed to too much sun. Other than that minor discomfort, I felt great. I knew Dr. Kaufman was keeping an eye on results and my spirits soared. As the treatments progressed my hopes were on the rise. My family and I felt our prayers had been answered.

"Okay, Alan," Dr. Kaufman said, "now we'll have another look inside and see where we are." This time I welcomed the cystoscopy. I was sure it would show a clean bill of health. I was feeling great. Why not?

Again out of the anesthetic. This time the smiles were unconvincing. I braced myself for what I knew was coming. Dr. Kaufman was blunt. "Well, it was worth the try, but we lost. There were areas that could not be reached and we have to do the Bladder Resection."

"C'est la vie miserable," said I, trying to lift the weight that had suddenly begun pressing my heart.

Dr. Kaufman continued, "Dr. Govan and his radiologist were right, but you've had almost three months extra use of your bladder, and we know we gave it a good try. Actually, there was some regression, but not enough."

"So let's get it over with," I [said in a low voice]. "When?"

"Day after tomorrow...we'll have to get you ready."

As I looked into Dr. Kaufman's eyes just before the operation began, I was filled with confidence. I knew that for the next six hours all of the energies of one of the top urological surgeons in the entire world would be directed in my behalf. I went to sleep, smiling.

"It's not working, it's not working!" seeped into my numbed brain.

"I can't figure out what I did wrong." This in Dr. Kaufman's far away voice. Then the overpowering, heart-sinking despair as I faded in and out of consciousness...DOOMED...Doomed... Doom...

Then that wonderful third day morning in Intensive Care! I'm sure the reader can now see the double impact of those lovely words.... "YABBA DABBA DOO!...It's working!"

What had not been working for two days was that there had been no flow of fluid from the stoma, despite the fact that I had been given as much water to drink as I could hold. It had taken those first two days for my body to accept the change.

But then suddenly everything was all right. And it's been all right ever since. And now every time Dr. Kaufman reassures me that I'm "clean as a whistle," I let forth with a loud, but ever so grateful, "YABBA DABBA DOO!"

It wasn't *all* Flintstones in later life for Reed. One of the strangest projects came from the animated world again in *Shinbone Alley*, a musical feature (written by Joe Darion and Mel Brooks) from the infamous Archy & Mehitabel stories by Don Marquis. Archy (voiced by Eddie Bracken) is a newspaper man reincarnated in the body of a cockroach, yet still with the insatiable desire to write poetry to the promiscuous cat he loves, Mehitable (Carol Channing). The trouble is, the latest of Mehitable's many loves is Big Bill (Alan Reed), a one-eyed big butch cat who sounds and acts as tough as he looks, especially to poor Archy who only tries to save the frisky cat from herself. It's a love/hate relationship between roach and feline, but all is forgiven on Mehitable's part when she reluctantly has kittens and is forced to settle down.

Shinbone Alley showcased Alan's Flintstone voice again, but was worlds away from the "safe" situations of *The Flintstones*. It's a very adult cartoon, much more so than those with "adult humor" like *Bullwinkle*, tackling such lofty "child" subjects such as war, sexuality, unwanted children, and life after death. Regardless, it's a fascinating, stylish, simple-yet-sketchy animated feature that has thankfully been uncovered with a long-awaited DVD release. Alan even gets to sing the title song,

> *Now down in Shinbone Alley;*
> *we're the toughest kinda cat.*
> *We play a little baseball;*
> *use our tails for bats.*

He also joins in on the "Home, Sweet Home" song playing over the end credits.

Alan's last film, and possibly his biggest role (at least in terms of screen time) was *The Seniors* (1978), a sex comedy about four college guys (Lou Richards, Dennis Quaid, Gary Imhoff, Jeffrey Byron)

The students are so frightened of getting boring jobs and losing their live-in nymphomaniac Sylvia (Priscilla Barnes) that they desperately concoct a way of getting as much fun out of their last year as they can. Using Professor Heigner (Alan Reed) and his sex experiments on mosquitoes as a front in order to get grant money, the four brazen lads solicit college women for a "sex study," paying them $20 an hour on a strictly "sex for science" basis. But the plot, like the college guys, is more ambitious—they get the smart idea that if they branch out, and let some business men who can afford donations for "research" have a go at the willing ladies, they'll be able to grow as a business and save for their future (i.e. making the scheme last years, not just the remaining five months of college they have left). Making $72k in just a day leads them to go into partnership with a seedy

banker who helps them grow into an empire by suggesting more partners (a bishop, the police commissioner, etc.), and soon the young men are selling stock in their research organization to a cosmetic firm for $10 million so they can push all the young ladies toward their line of useful feminine hygiene products.

Meantime, poor Prof. Heigner (a three-time Nobel Prize winner who admits "it should've been four — I was cheated") is stalked by the sex-starved virgin, Miss Creighton (Lynn Cartwright), whose grant money started this whole thing. She keeps sneaking into his lab and reading his notes on the amazing conquests of his super mosquito, assuming that the professor is the one who can go from partner to partner with amazing stamina. When she confronts him, he mistakenly admits that (as far as working on research goes, he means) "I can go five, six hours a day. With a nap, maybe seven or eight hours. The secret is keep *pushing!*" But Heigner only lives for research. "The mosquito is more honorable than the human," says he. "He will not talk of love when he is thinking of sex." But not knowing a gnat about mosquitoes, frenzied Miss Creighton gets worked up into a terrible state when she professes utter love for the 70+ year old.

"Take me!"

"Take you where?"

"I'm begging for sex!"

"You are begging from a *poor* man…"

It was a great showcase for Reed, and with his lighter German accent, it never once made you think of Fred. But the film's clever ideas were often thwarted by its lack of a completely coherent script. There were plenty of familiar faces mixed into its starring and supporting cast, but the tone and acting was far too *Porky's* for its day (perhaps), without the actual gloss of a *Meatballs* budget.

Alan Reed, Jr. recalled, "The Seniors — *wow. It was the last picture Dad did, released after he died. I was given a videocassette of it soon after its release and I couldn't (didn't) watch it until a year or two ago. I knew he must have looked terrible and didn't want to remember Dad that way in a raunchy little sex comedy. Seeing him physically wasn't easy, but I did enjoy the performance — in spite of the silly movie itself.*

"It was shot in late 1976 or early 1977. Dad was in very poor health, feeling lousy, when he got a call from the movie's director Rod Amateau [the former director of television's Love That Bob*]. He wasn't happy with the casting and really wanted Dad to do it. Worried that he wasn't up to it, Dad was very reluctant. He would be needed in Dallas for one or two weeks. Rod assured him that with Mom accompanying him and the best arrangements possible, he'd love it and be great. Well, Mom was with him every step of the way, on set and off, and though I don't know if he loved it, he gave it his all. And to discover that thirty years later made me as proud as ever of my Pop."*

Alan's last years saw him in failing health, but active to the end. As Alan Reed, Jr. remembered, *"He had not been well for several months with periodic hospital stays for two-three days at a time. He was scheduled for another check-in on a Tuesday in early June, 1977. He learned he was needed for a Flintstones session that morning and, with less than full energy, agreed to do it. Mom took him to the studio and, when recording completed, to the hospital. We all expected it to be another brief stay as before. But that was not to be. Things turned for the worse, and he passed away in the hospital a few days later. Not a happy story but one we all remember well. And his memorial service at our family home the following Sunday, Father's Day, was an unexpectedly cheerful occasion full of many happy stories and fond remembrances from those who loved him."*

Alan Reed died on June 14, 1977, leaving behind a loving family, and a legacy that will never be forgotten.

Appendix

I. MISCELLANEOUS WRITINGS

This short piece was written about Alan's mother-in-law, near the end her life.

"My Mother-In-Law"
by Alan Reed

She had led a most adventurous life. Born at Rice Lake, Wisconsin, on the ranch her pioneer parents had homesteaded, she'd had to ride horseback six miles a day to and from school. At 16 she pumped a railroad handcar every Saturday to get to a dance 15 miles down the track. At 22, while a nurse in San Francisco, she evacuated her bedridden patients during the earthquake of 1906.

Married to a mining engineer, she trekked to the interior of Nicaragua when she was four months pregnant — and back out when her first child, Finette, was born. Her two other children, Robert and Margaret, were born 14,500 feet high at the Cerro de Pasco mine in Peru.

It was a life guided by frugality and self-discipline. Widowed, she worked, scrimped, saved and invested until she was able to tell her children proudly, "Now, I'll never have to be a burden to you." And that pride makes her present condition doubly poignant.

She is now 87, white-haired, stooped and hesitant, and she repeats many times a day, "Oh, I'm so ashamed" — for there remains just enough awareness of her increasing senility with its accompanying mental deterioration to keep her constantly embarrassed. She goes from complete lucidity to a lack of awareness of surroundings in a matter of seconds.

Knowing what she was, we love her the more for what she is — Vitaline Pijean Walker, my mother-in-law.

As Alan Reed, Jr. explains, *"The following is a letter from my father to his brother-in-law, William C. Hunt (my uncle Bill) who was married to Margaret (Aunt Peggy), my mother's younger sister. The letter was written in 1971-72 and gives an idea of Dad's thinking and some of the things that were important to him."*

Tuesday afternoon

Dear Bill,

A most interesting article — especially the De Gaulle-Kissinger-Nixon entente. Also the reference to the five-power world of Metternich. However, my opinion of Nixon (even tho he seems to be after a different foreign policy) will never change. I know him for an opportunist who will use any means *that he can get away with* to further his own ends.

All politicians must have something of this quality in order to survive — but I've seen an early Nixon performance in California that nauseated me.

A very true truism on "all politicians" comes through an old joke. It can be updated by having the question asked: "What's the difference between Nixon and Muskie?" The answer is: "Picture both as babies sitting on your lap — one on each knee. They'll both piss on you — but the one who smiles will be Nixon."

Bill, I am working very hard, making speeches at membership drive events for "Common Cause." Primarily, because I don't think our basic problems can be assured until there are changes in our government. I don't mean change of administration — I mean new hard and fast laws to make our government more responsive to that vogue group which is all of us — "the people."

There is too much concentration of power in too few individuals and corporation — through their ability to lobby — to finance the "right" campaigns, and to keep control of key decision making committees through the seniority system.

Common Cause is the nearest thing to a "People's Lobby" that we have today. Its aims and actions are dictated by its membership (now 250,000). The members are polled twice a year (via questionnaire) for their priorities in projects — and an *elected* board proceeds to move as directed. An overwhelming majority chose as its first preference — government change. Disclosure of *all* campaign contributions accompanied by a constant publication of how *every* Congressman and Senator votes on each issue — Pointing up, when and where necessary, the correlation of vote and contribution. The organization is growing and is now moving into state and regional activity. Of course, there are many other needs that we will go after — but we have wisely (I think) decided not to dissipate our value by spreading too thin. The overall objective requires patience.

I think the most important contribution that can be made to our country at this time in our history is to awaken our people from the terrible apathy that really prevents our achieving our heritage. If Common Cause can grow to a million members who are constant, I think that goal can be attained. Anyway, it's a good feeling to be able to do some small battle for something you believe in — So much for politics.

My writing studies are progressing. I think I've digested the basics — now I'm just beginning to outline the direction of my book. It's a monumental job just getting ready to start getting ready to write. I do a few exercises — searching for a style. I don't remember if I've ever sent you any of my stuff. I'm enclosing some, including a recent treatise on Death. I'm fascinated by this subject and I plan to enlarge the scope of this short piece into a full-fledged article. Let's have a reaction, eh?

Hope this finds you all well.

Goombye
T

• • •

Alan Reed, Jr.: *"This is a letter Dad wrote in 1971 to Roy Pigeon, my mother's cousin. It recounts some colorful things about the early life of my grandmother, Vital, Dad's mother-in-law. She was a remarkable woman, coming from pioneer stock, and it's evident how much Dad loved and admired her."*

March 11, 1971

Dear Roy,

It's just about a month since I received your warm, friendly letter. I've meant to answer sooner but I've been busy on a new project. Although we've never met I've thought of you on occasion and of the quiet, but to me, interesting life you lead in the "cold country." You are the last male survivor of the Pigeon family.

Ever since a trip to Eureka, Montana, which we took with our three boys and Vital (Aunt Vitaline) about 25 years ago — I've been most interested in the Pigeon family. Interested, of course, because of my wife's antecedents, but also because they represented a kind of life which I had always admired but never knew. My family were New York City dwellers ever since my grandfather came here from Russia in 1883. Well, on that trip we saw the homestead site of the Pigeon ranch, we crossed the Pigeon Bridge and visited your grandmother's grave. We also met an old gentleman who was then the Sheriff of Libby, Montana. This gent used to court Vital when he was a young man. He told us an interesting tale — Once a month he would pick up Vital (who was then 16 or 17) and would take her to a dance at a railroad junction 15 miles away. What made it interesting was the way they got to the junction. Vital would be dressed in a long white organdy dress, which would blow lustily in the breeze as they proceeded 15 miles down the railroad tracks — both of them standing and PUMPING A HAND CAR!

We had arranged by phone to meet the Sheriff in the lobby of the Libby Hotel (sounds like a song title: "LOBBY OF THE LIBBY"). When we got to the hotel, our son Steve (then 8, now 32) ran in alone ahead of us. The Sheriff took one look at him and said, "My God — it's Billy Pigeon!" He told us that Steve looked exactly like your Uncle Billy when *he* was a little boy.

At that time Vital was 61 — and on the road to Eureka, she pointed out the hill from which she first saw the Pigeon ranch in Montana…fifty years before. You see, when the family left Buckley, Washington they left the two girls behind at a convent school in Seattle. Later, when Aunt Finette was 13 and Vital was 11, her brothers (your uncles Walter and Billy) went back to Seattle and brought the girls home to the new ranch in Montana…that was 75 years ago. They came by train to Jennings and then by horseback (about sixty miles) to the ranch at what is now Eureka. Those were hardy times.

When we got to Eureka we stayed at a farm owned by a girlhood friend of Vital's — Jessie Morrison (also 61). And, to my amazement, they had a spirited race on horseback —what a gal. I've got movies of it and of the old ranch site and the Pigeon Bridge and your grandmother's gravestone. I'll show them to you when you can get down here. You see Roy, I'm a city feller and as such, I'm much impressed with the hardihood of the rugged frontier life. Vital is now 86 and in remarkable physical condition. Mentally, she goes in and out. Sometimes she's perfectly normal and the next minute she might not know where she is. She's not really senile (Aunt Finette is), it's just that her brain plays tricks on her. She has my undying respect. She's really earned the right to be cared for.

You'll notice I put an asterisk alongside of the name FINETTE—a name seemingly exclusive to the Pigeons and their descendants. In case you don't know — it's of French origin — derived from the flower…Delphinium which brought about the name DELPHINE and FINETTE is the diminutive or pet name…the "ette" meaning "little." So literally it means "Little Flower." My gal's baptismal name was RUTH DELPHINE.

As I've said, we've been married for 39 years after we met in New York where Finette had come for a singing career. I first saw her in 1931 over a closed channel television viewer. Yes, way back then CBS was experimenting with TV. Finette was singing and I was waiting to follow her on the rudimentary equipment they then called television. We were married 6 months later. We've been most fortunate in raising a family that is close and loving. Our boys have married fine women and we all live within 25 minutes of each other. We get together more often (I think) than the average family — there is love and we are grateful.

Finette will be 62 in June and I'll be 64 in August. I've been an actor most of my life, working as such in Radio, Television, Motion Pictures and the Theatre. I've been fairly successful — never becoming a "Star" but working regularly and gaining some small recognition. For the past ten years I've been associated with a TV cartoon series which has become a very big, long lasting success. It's been shown in most countries around the world but I don't know if it's ever been seen in Canada. It's called "THE FLINTSTONES" and I am the voice of the leading character, FRED FLINTSTONE. Seventeen years ago I started the business described on the letterhead and I've just passed it on to my son Christopher who has done much to build it. He's a whiz of a salesman.

Well Roy, that brings you up to date (sketchily) on our end of the family. Finette and Vital both join me in inviting you to visit us when you can. We haven't as large a house as we did when your Uncle Walter visited us, but we'll try to make you comfortable. Let's hear from you.

Best regards,
Alan Reed

• • •

Alan Reed, Jr.: *"I don't have a date on Dad's 'Looking Forward' poem, but I'm sure it was in his last year or two. He always believed in God as the original originator and was fascinated by the Eternal Mystery. His thoughts in the poem about the answer only coming after death had been expressed to us often through the years. The somewhat formal structure of the poem suggests it was written as part of his writing course."*

"Looking Forward"

Will it be Nothingness
Or the revelation of the GREAT UNANSWERED?

I am curious!

Throughout life have I sought basic truths —
Yet the BASIC BASIC has eluded me.
Neither Logic, Science nor Religion
Has provided the ultimate answer.

Logic, to which I owe first allegiance,
Tells me there must be an Ordered Plan.

Science begins with a whirling VOID.
But Logic asks: "Why was it whirling?"

Religion and its answers
Call for an unswerving Faith
Which provides a Belief...truly *believed.*
But in equal truth...not truly *known.*

In all of the life of Man
Not one *indisputable* sign
Has come from the ORIGINATOR!

Religion will cry:
"Was not JESUS resurrected
To give truth to HIS words?
And if you will not follow the MASTER
You will never KNOW."

Logic answers: "Think again of *believe* and KNOW!"
Think of the relative few who were Witnesses
to what *mortal man* has transcribed as Gospel.

Religion replies: "He who rejects the LORD
Cannot know the TRUTH."

Yet Logic persists...he answers:

"By that very statement you invest
The Greatness shown in all Creation and Reproduction
With the human frailty of petty peevishness.

Surely one cannot conceive
The Great Mind of the Universe
Equating with the childlike words...
'If you don't play my way, you can't play at all!'"

NO!

That is beyond Logic's acceptance.

Certainly, if HE or IT or FORCE or WHAT YOU WILL
wished us to know, *at this stage* of our existence,
HE would convince emphatically, again and again
Till no single doubter be left!

So the Great Question...What After?
Is only answered (if answered at all)
By DEATH.

So...*Hoping* for the answer...
I look forward....to Death.

II. FRED ALLEN'S LETTERS TO ALAN REED

Fred Allen wrote Alan several letters (purposely all typed in lower case), which are reprinted here with the kind permission of the Boston Public Library.

march 12th, 1945

dear alan...

your man, mr. griesedick, sounds like a composite fellow who boasts all of the petty traits and horseshit charm that i have coped with among my executive superiors for the past twelve years. it seems in every organization there lurks a puffed jerk, with two cents of authority and an inbred desire to make some actor's life miserable. in radio these cruds are obviously successful as a look at any comedian, or person heading a program, will confirm. if it isn't the rating it's the comedy, if it isn't the comedy it's the music and if it isn't the music it's the announcer who isn't dragging out the commercials so that they dominate the show. your rating, with the limited coverage and the time, is swell. if you had a seven or eight on a network show, around here, with the cost of your show you could probably tell brother g what to do with his beer bottles.

am glad that you bought that house. in that section i think it is a good investment. properties hold their value in beverly and later on if you wanted to unload it to go elsewhere you can probably make a small profit on the manse. i don't think the fact that john and charlie are landowners in that area will have any immediate effect on values. if you keep inviting charlie out to hillcrest to impersonate a pigeon you'll have him back working on those morning shows. charlie told me he liked it out there with the car and the golf course so handy and i hear john on the half hour practically so i know he must be happy.

i made a lot of transcriptions for columbia recently and wrote minnie into all of them. she has been working with ed wynn but the show went off last week and i don't know what she is doing. i am on the hall of fame in a couple of weeks and am going to call her and see if she wants to work on that. i don't know too much about radio around here but it seems to be pretty tired. as you know most of the top shows are out there so there isn't too much activity here. i have been doing a few guest shots and some magazine pieces along with the transcriptions which have kept me busy. i have a lot of offers for next season and may do the show again. i am to be examined again in may and if my pressure has gone down any and the doctor thinks i can stand another season of drudgery i may get going. i'll let you know what happens later. after taxes, there is so little money left that i am better off doing a few guest shots. when i think of mark sandrich, dave freedman, danny donker and some of the others i am tempted to quit the whole thing and do something else for a while.

when "nob hill" comes out, if the cutting room hasn't undone you again you will probably get some action from the studios. i saw our picture [*It's in the Bag!*] and it isn't too hot in my estimation. the opening has some laughs and there are some good scenes with jack benny and the others but the picture isn't near as good as it should have been.

the great problem in hollywood is to keep occupied. there is too much time to sit around in the sun. you are fortunate with the program and camps to keep you going since that is the most important thing. around here there are so many shows and things to do that even when you're not working the time passes pleasantly. out there, entertainment is so scarce that you have to make your own. you see the same people everyplace and the cast system determines your associates. if you happen to be a big hit in a picture you suddenly have a new set of acquaintances. i know a lot of people like it but for some reason it all bores me and i prefer the new york routine.

i have heard a lot of cologne jokes but yours was really the best. the other writers all had to get stinker in with odor but your line had dignity that is as much dignity as a joke involving smell can have. it was okay.

the curfew has loused up the nightclub business and all of the shows, except the hits, have dropped their grosses. i rewrote two bits for "the voices" and am working with franky boy this wednesday. h. allen smith wants me to write a book. it seems like a lot of work which i am loath to start. i have turned all of my business over to the morris office and between brother lastfogel and mr. william murray i will probably have plenty to do if i don't fall apart.

hope that finette and the tribe are all well. if there is anything i can do for you here...let me know. hope "nob hill" turns out okay and that your sponsor will co-operate with the recordings. if anything develops out there...keep me informed especially if the boxers are boxing, the machines is going, etc.

best wishes,
f.a.
180 west 58th

april 21st [1945]

dear alan...

i have been exposed to so much commotion i haven't had time to get at the mail-outgoing. last week, i started on a tour to make several towns where the picture was to open. i got as far as washington and baltimore when the president died and the balance of the junket was cancelled. when i returned minnie wanted to go with a uso unit overseas but had no vehicle. i was engaged on the cuff to conjure up some sort of a routine that would serve min. for this purpose. you will be glad to learn that miss pious has just left my workshop with the first draft of her monologue and she is quite happy. after she has played a few dates we are to confer again and remedy any defects to make her specialty surefire.

last week, i spoke at the peabody award dinner and next week i am leaving for boston to arrange and speak at a school dinner honoring the principal who is retiring in june. with all of my dinner speeches i am getting to be known as the gentile jessel and i will be able to give georgie a run for honors in this field with a little more experience.

you can see that my days are crowded and i am almost as busy as when i had the show to grind out every week. the only difference is that i make my own hours and do not have to function under pressure. yesterday, i had a blood pressure session and my systolic and diastolic pressures were lower than they have been for five years. i think the secret of the whole thing is to quit working. you have to have another secret to go with the first secret though and that is a secret that will enable you to find a way to live without working.

i think you are fortunate to be finished with brother griesedick. that show served its purpose and continuing with the aggravation stirred up by brother g for another year would have given you a set of ulcers or something. the personal appearance dates in those cities is a swell idea. you tell stories as well as anyone i know and with a short routine, a few good stories and a poem or so you should be set for any theatre dates you want to play. i haven't been in a vaudeville theatre for fifteen years. last week, down in washington, i was horsed into working one show with jimmy dorsey. i had to hustle to get a routine together and was amazed at the reaction the material got from the jitterbug audience. in those theatres they have seen so many of those alleged band comedians that any performer with a solid routine and some talent to sell it is a cinch to do well. i hope you get the dates for i know you would have a lot of fun around

those towns and it is good for you personally to get around and be seen by audiences and also to meet people we never see staying in n.y. and hollywood.

the hall of fame show was assembled in a hurry and your rural relative was the only character available. i could have put a few bars of "yankee doodle" in to go with the "wait for me, fellers" but i didn't think of it. you are right about smart's beard. it is off but his hair is now dyed a patent leather black to enable him to play a native in "bell for adano." patsy we got from his sun-chair on the roof of the edison and his dialect might have sounded a little blistered. it seemed funny to do an hour again and i would hate to have it hanging over my head for another 39 weeks.

wish you would let me know your plans later. i have a lot of offers and next month i may make a deal for the fall. you are right about most of the agency heads. with the great dearth of talent in radio you would think that they would attempt to line up a few actors with ability and build shows around them. i guess, though, that this requires too much effort. if they unload me on a client they can sit back and grab the commission and i can go worry about where the jokes are coming from for the season. at the peabody award dinner last week, john royal spoke on the shortage of new talent and intimated that radio had a great problem for the future. i had already spoken so i couldn't very well jump up again in rebuttal and say "why don't you guys look around and do something for the talented people you have on the networks."

hope you still like hollywood. george levy was here a few weeks ago and said that he saw you at hillcrest [country club] a lot. i like it there for a short stay but i still maintain that it is more stimulating around here. there are too many clicks [cliques] and you have to play politics out there to survive. i think the sun bakes the good out of many of the people the same as it dries the land. i would rather have hunger pains in front of lindy's than to be found belching inside of romanoff's. but to hell with it. what is one man's fish is another man's gefilte.

will let you know what happens to me when i return from boston around may 5th. if you run across charlie and john say hello. i saw john in jack benny's picture and i thought he was swell in his waiter bit. trust that finette is well and that you have pontoons on the kiddies now that the swimming pool season is about to open.

i am still dizzy. the pacers are trotting, the fighters are firking, etc.

regards....
f.a.

may 6th [1945]

dear alan...

received a letter from charles (pigeon) cantor this morning. his missive reminded me that i owed you a quota of chit-chat. have been in the hospital the past two weeks and my mail is all buggered up. my parotid gland was infected. the doctor put me in for one night to give me 200,000 units of penicillin. i was supposed to leave for boston the next day to speak at a school dinner. the next day, i awakened to find my head looking like an old basketball that someone had let a little air out of and it took the better part of two weeks before my head went down to 12 ½ so that i could get it through the door to get out of the hospital room. the shrinking continued until my head went down to around a 4 ¾ size. fortunately, i have the name of the woman who used to make walter tetley's caps, years ago, and i am getting small denim caps made up. that penicillin is great stuff. they inject it into the posteriors. after about twenty shots with the needle you go to sleeping feeling as though a male porcupine is mounting you.

you will be glad to learn that minnie tried out her act at the merchant marine canteen last week. the u.s.c. heads were there and all approved of her monologue, her physical has been passed and after some shots it looks as though min will be winging her way overseas to become the life of the fox-hole. that "gunnery" story was swell. i will tell it to her when she reports later. i am trying to get her to play a couple of hospitals or camps to do the routine a few times to get familiar with it and to find the weak gags so that they can be replaced before she takes off.

abe burrows wrote me that he was leaving ed [Duffy's Tavern]. i think it will be a good thing for him. you can't keep grinding out those shows year after year and not have something happen to you. abe said he had a couple of clever boys working on the shows and ed knows what he wants so that abe isn't leaving him a headache. i heard you playing the western louse on the greenwood show sunday — during my stay in the hospital and since i have had to stay in i have been catching a lot of programs i never knew existed before. if the personal appearance dates are off you ought to grab some of that dough in radio. none of the shows mean anything and a dollar you don't catch in radio today is gone forever. a radio reputation means nothing unless it can get a person some extra dough in pictures or theatres. john brown will probably end up better off than amos and andy without any of the responsibility. radio is the creepiest and most unimportant branch of the profession thespians have been forced to cope with to date.

if you do go to chicago for the barn dance dates perhaps i can see you if you come to new york. may 22nd i have to go to boston to help arrange a school dinner but i'll be back here june 1st. i think around the last week in june we will go up to maine. abe lastfogel came in town last week and we are going to make some sort of a deal for the fall. once that is settled i will disappear artistically until it comes time to assemble a banner cast and writing staff later on. will let you know what happens when the thing is consummated.

have been thinking about the pool problem in beverly. a lot of those houses, like charlie's, haven't room enough in back to accommodate a pool. if you could go around the neighborhood with a portable pool you might make a lot of money. if charlie is entertaining mort lewis anticipating a couple of shots on the billie burke show. he doesn't want mort to know that he has no pool. this could bring the salary down to scale. charlie calls you up the night before. you show up early in the morning with your portable pool. you fit it into charlie's yard and when mort looks out the window he is impressed. with a pool, not too large, one that you could travel with easily, i think you would clean up out there this summer. you could get a guarantee as lifeguard and perhaps train a gull or two to fly over the pool on cue to give sort of a picturesque touch to the rental. this is starting to sound good to me. if you know where i can get some water cheap and a wet hole to put it in i might start renting my pool around bel air which would not conflict with your territory. let me know how this sounds. do you want to let harry green in for a piece. anyone taking a piece in the pool would be cautioned, of course.

to hell with this. we have a potroast on the table. where we got it i don't know. perhaps portland listened to the bendix show for ten consecutive sundays. if you do i think the american meat institute sends you a potroast. but it is on the table and i have got to lam.

hope the finette and all are well. if there is anything i can do for you here...let me know. outside of digging up some laughs for my after-dinner speech in boston i am practically unemployed the next two weeks. port joins me in sending best wishes...

F.A.
180 west 58th

may 21st [1945]

dear alan...

your letter came this a.m. i am leaving for boston tomorrow to spend about ten days at bond rallies and ending up at a school alumni dinner as toastmaster. i wanted to send you a few lines before i left.

you are right about the hollywood setup. i know it would be a lot better but we have some problems here. my brother has been in and out of the hospital the past four years. he is in again this week for further observation and in his condition i don't want to work too far away from boston in the immediate future. all of portland's family are here and as you know that place gets me down. if things change, later on, perhaps we can come out there but i will have to start the season here.

your future is definitely out there. all you need is one decent break in pictures and you can forget about radio. charlie [cantor] and john [brown] should be all set out there. as long as radio pimps on the picture industry, and it appears that it will for years to come, most of the shows will be out there and naturally work will be more profitable there and living a lot easier, too. while you are waiting for pictures you can make all you want in radio so you have a triple reason to make hollywood your base...i threw in finette and the juniors.

i'll let you know what happens later. we are not making any commitments until around labor day. i just asked the morris office to contact you before we did anything.

saw min at the uso office today where she was rehearsing. she tried her routine out again at a camp last friday and everything went okay. as the author i called and we have some sports to fix up but she is going to play a few more hospitals and camps near here and do the routine so that she knows where the laughs are and where the boffs need vulcanizing. she is all enthused about going overseas and the unit is rehearsing so it looks as though she will be gone in a week or two.

saw nat and mandy yesterday. they had just had a small "peen" session and i think a few spritzers were consummated during the play. nat expects to go overseas shortly for a trip on air forces assignment. he isn't sure about it. he was leaving for washington this morning to write some shows down there and then he'll know what they intend to do with him in a week, or two.

will write you when i get back from boston. i think you should grab what looks best for you and if something comes up later we can work it out some day to our mutual advantage. you don't owe me anything. in this racket opportunities come unexpectedly and a day and a dollar lost may not be trapped again.

hope all goes well. best wishes...

f.a. 180 west 58

august 26th 1945

dear alan...

your letter was forwarded up here to maine arriving yesterday.
it's funny. earlier this week i had a letter from joe moran, at young
& rubican's, saying that they expected you to start with ed on the
duffy show. joe wanted to know if the falstaff character was copy-
righted and if i had given you permission to do it on other programs.
i told him that i had given you an okay to portray the lovable louse
and thought that the deal was set.

now i am sort of screwed up. at your suggestion we made a
deal with irving kaufman and we also have three others, including
minnie, and i won't be able to figure out what i can do until i get
back to the city.

i don't know whether it would be good to open with falstaff and
then have a let-down when you had to go back and we had to start
to build up some other character or characters. it might be better
for us to try to get under way with whatever we have and then later,
when you had some time, we could make the falstaff appearance
more important as a guest visit.

don't let me futz up anything you have on the fire out there. we
are supposed to have a meeting sept. 15th to decide on the first few
shows. as soon as i got things straightened out i will let you know
what i can do wangling things around. will wire you as near as the
15th as i can. if you are tied up we can work something out later. it
will work out okay one way or another.

am not surprised that the minions at the morris office have had
you baffled. i went up there one day before we left and couldn't even
get in to see mr. jordan. i had to sit around in the outer office until
one of the boys came in and rescued me. i wouldn't be surprised if
one of the new employees let mr. lastfogel or bill murray out some
day and then the organization will explode with a bang.

nat hiken is now a father, had a baby girl last week. nat expects
to go to the coast to see his daughter. you may bump into him cad-
dying at hillcrest tonight out there.

min is with a uso unit around the panama canal someplace.
i don't know how she has been doing as most of the troops in
the areas she has played have been natives and dutch. i thought
she was going to germany and we fixed up a routine that would
have been okay for american kids but god knows what has happened in puerto rico, brazil and panama where min has been on
exhibition.

hope finette and the young are still enthused about california. i owe charlie cantor a letter which i hope to get off this week. i spent a couple of weeks in bed here with more mumps but i think i will outlast sinatra as i feel okay now. will be back at 180 west 58th sept. 5th and will wire you on above date or sooner if i can.

regards,
f. allen

january 1st 1949

teddy —

thanx a lot for the "blum and adler" gag. i will use it in one of min's routines the first chance i get. it is perfect for her and as you may suspect i am getting numb after about ten years of writing those bon mots.

if you want to come here any week around the end of january or during february, with the exception of feb. 13th week, i will tell wallie jordan to send you a contract for a grand. i will write some kind of a spot and take the dough out of the guest spot. will have to grab off a cut-rate guest that week but if i know a couple of weeks in advance i can get someone.

television is creating a lot of talk around the agencies and in the gossip columns but there are only a couple of shows that pay any money. the agency minds forgot that most of the television sets are in and around new york and one or two other cities. it will be three or four years before enough sets are out to really undermine radio. from the looks of most of the television entertainment it will probably kill itself off before it ruins radio. all i can tell you is that the top show is milton berle doing a smalltime vaudeville show with ed wynn additions to the show. berle has grabbed everything wynn ever had and when he runs out of what he has stolen down through the years he will be in trouble. when berle gets to himself, in other words, television will scale new depths.

let me know about the date. hope everything is okay. regards to charlie if you ever see him around. happy new year.

fred allen
180 west 58

Credits

RADIO

Compiled by Martin Grams, Jr. with assistance from Jack French, Terry Salomonson and Karl Schadow

November 16, 1926 - December 16, 1930 *The Eveready Hour*
Variety program. Among the cast during these years were Richard Dix, Eddie Cantor, Belle Baker, Lionel Atwill and Alan Reed. Sponsored by the National Carbon Company for Eveready Batteries. NBC.

Circa 1927 - April 17, 1932 *The Collier Hour*
Dramatic anthology program, used to promote *Collier's* magazine. Many were adaptations of stories that appeared within the magazine's issues. Cast included Jack Arthur, Phil Barrison and Alan Reed. Blue Network.

May 16, 1929 - May 8, 1930 *True Detective Mysteries*
(also known as *True Detective Stories*) Anthology series of mystery dramas, sponsored by MacFadden Publications with adaptations from short stories in their magazines. Jack Shuttleworth narrated. Alan Reed was among the cast. CBS.

Circa 1930s Syndicated *Meyer the Buyer*
Comedy program with Harry Hershfield. Exact dates varied across the country because the series was syndicated, which meant various local stations could air the program on their own time, with local sponsors. Alan Reed was among the cast.

April 14, 1930 - January 26, 1931 *Believe-It-Or-Not*

Weekly regular: Robert L. Ripley. This hour-hour program featured a song or two, and a number of trivial and dramatic skits with Alan Reed occasionally supplying a voice-over or performing a supporting role for a few of those skits. Sponsored by Colonial Oil. NBC.

July 31, 1930 - July 30, 1931 *Detective Story Hour*

Weekly regular: James La Curto (Frank Readick as of October 23, 1930) This half-hour anthology featured stories from current issues of Street and Smith's Detective Story Magazine. Alan Reed played a lead or supporting role in almost every broadcast of the series. CBS.

December 27, 1930 - July 29, 1931 *The Palmolive Hour*

This hour-long program was an anthology of stories ranging from romance to mystery. Alan Reed played a supporting role in a large number of episodes. Sponsored by Palmolive. NBC.

May 20, 1931 - February 12, 1932 *Believe It or Not*

Weekly regular: Robert L. Ripley. This 15-minute program was broadcast twice a week (Wednesday and Friday) and featured a song or two, and a number of trivial and dramatic skits with Alan Reed occasionally supplied a voice-over or performed a supporting role. Sponsored by Esso. Blue Network.

September 6, 1931 - October 11, 1931 *Blue Coal Radio Revue*

Weekly regular: Frank Readick. This hour-long program featured a half hour of music and a half-hour mystery drama from current issues of Street and Smith magazines. Alan Reed played a lead or supporting role in almost every broadcast of the series. CBS.

September 13, 1931 - January 31, 1932 *The Chase and Sanborn Hour*

Weekly regular: Eddie Cantor. This hour-long program featured a half hour of music and a half hour of variety, which included songs, skits and dramas performed by Cantor and a supporting cast (including Alan Reed), and a few of Cantor's songs. Reed played supporting roles for a number of skits. NBC. Known existing recordings: December 13, 1931.

October 1, 1931 - October 8, 1931 *Love Story Drama*

Weekly regular: Frank Readick. This half-hour program featured a romance drama from current issues of Street and Smith's Love Story magazines. Alan Reed played a lead or supporting role in both broadcasts. CBS.

October 15, 1931 - September 22, 1932 *Love Story Hour*
Weekly regular: Frank Readick. This half-hour program featured a romance drama from current issues of Street and Smith's Love Story magazines. Alan Reed played a lead or supporting role in almost all of the broadcasts. CBS.

October 25, 1931 - March 13, 1932 *Blue Coal Radio Revue*
Weekly regular: Frank Readick. This hour-long program featured a half hour of music and a half-hour mystery drama from current issues of Street and Smith magazines. Alan Reed played a lead or supporting role in almost every broadcast of the series. CBS.

October 30, 1931 - April 23, 1933 *The Chase and Sanborn Hour*
Weekly regular: Eddie Cantor. This hour-long program featured a half hour of music and a half hour of variety, which included songs, skits and dramas performed by Cantor and a supporting cast (including Alan Reed). NBC.

November 2, 1931 - May 27, 1932 *Myrt and Marge*
(also known as *The Story of Myrt and Marge*) Soap opera about a seasoned chorus girl and her crime-fighting husband, a district attorney. Myrtle Vail, Vinton Hayworth and Donna Damerel were regulars. Alan Reed, Santos Ortega and Ed Begley were among the actors playing a number of recurring characters. Five-times-a-week, 15 minutes. Sponsored by Wrigley. CBS.

January 5, 1932 - February 2, 1932 *The Shadow*
Weekly regular: Frank Readick. This half-hour program featured mystery dramas adapted from Street and Smith mystery magazines. Alan Reed played a lead or supporting role in all five broadcasts. Sponsored by Hachmeister Lind Co. CBS.

April 3, 1932 - June 26, 1932 *The Jack Pearl Show*
Comedy and variety program. Cliff Hall was a regular. Alan Reed participated in a few of the dramatic sketches, but exactly which episodes remains unknown. Sponsored by Chrysler. CBS.

April 3, 1932 - June 5, 1932 *Blue Coal Radio Revue*
Weekly regular: Frank Readick. This hour-long program featured a half hour of music and a half-hour mystery drama from current issues of Street and Smith magazines. Alan Reed played a lead or supporting role in almost every broadcast of the series. CBS.

April 12, 1932 - August 16, 1932 *Joe Palooka*
Comedy thriller based on the comic strip by Ham Fisher. Alan Reed plays
the title role, described as an "amiable, dim-witted champion of the ring, the
store clerk who fights his way to the heavyweight championship of the world."
Sponsored by Heinz Rice Flakes. 15-minute program broadcast twice a week,
Tuesday and Thursday. CBS.

May 11, 1932 - June 6, 1932 *Believe It or Not*
Weekly regular: Robert L. Ripley. This 15-minute program was broadcast twice
a week (Wednesday and Friday) and featured a song or two, and a number of
trivial and dramatic skits with Alan Reed occasionally supplying a voice-over
or performing a supporting role. Sponsored by Esso. Blue Network.

July 19, 1932 - August 9, 1932 *Air Stories of the World War*
This short-run series lasted a mere four broadcasts, and included adaptations
of short stories from pulp magazines. Alan Reed plays supporting roles in at
least three of the four episodes. The series was syndicated, so the same four
episodes were heard on radio stations across the country as early as February 1932.

August 29, 1932 - January 1, 1937 *Myrt and Marge*
(also known as *The Story of Myrt and Marge*) Soap opera about a seasoned
chorus girl and her crime-fighting husband, a district attorney. Myrtle Vail,
Vinton Hayworth and Donna Damerel were regulars. Alan Reed, Santos
Ortega and Ed Begley were among the actors playing a number of recurring
characters. Five-times-a-week, 15 minutes. Sponsored by Wrigley. CBS.

September 8, 1932 - June 29, 1933 *The Lucky Strike Hour*
Comedy and variety program. Cliff Hall was a regular. Alan Reed participated in a few of the dramatic sketches, but exactly which episodes remains
unknown. Paul Whiteman supplied the music. Sponsored by Lucky Strike.
NBC.

October 2, 1932 - March 19, 1933 *Pages of Romance*
Serial drama. Alan Reed was among the cast. Sponsored by Fletcher's Cas-
toria. NBC.

October 5, 1932 - April 26, 1933 *Blue Coal Mystery Revue*
Weekly regular: Frank Readick. This half-hour program featured a mystery
drama from current issues of Street and Smith's mystery and detective magazines. Alan Reed played a lead or supporting role in most of the broadcasts.
Sponsored by D.L.&W. Coal Company. NBC.

October 23, 1932 - April 16, 1933 *The Linit Bath Club Revue*

Weekly regular: Fred Allen. This half-hour program featured a number of songs and comical skits with Alan Reed occasionally playing a supporting role. CBS.

November 7, 1932 - June 17, 1933 *Buck Rogers*

Science fiction serial starring Matt Crowley and Adele Ronson. Alan Reed is among the cast of supporting actors. Curtis Arnall replaced Matt Crowley after a few weeks. 15-minute series, five-times-a-week. Sponsored by Kellogg's. CBS.

April 30, 1933 - November 12, 1933 *The Bert Lahr Show*

This was a summer replacement for the Eddie Cantor program. Musical variety series with skits. Alan Reed was among the cast for most of the episodes. Sponsored by Chase and Sanborn. NBC.

August 4, 1933 - December 1, 1933 *The Salad Bowl Revue*

Weekly regular: Fred Allen. This half-hour program featured a number of songs and comical skits with Alan Reed occasionally playing a supporting role. NBC. Known Existing Recordings: September 8, 1933, October 6, 1933, October 20, 1933 and November 24, 1933.

October 2, 1933 - June 29, 1934 *Buck Rogers*

Science fiction serial starring Curtis Arnall and Adele Ronson. Alan Reed is among the cast of supporting actors. 15-minute series, four-times-a-week. Sponsored by Cocomalt. CBS.

October 7, 1933 - December 23, 1933 *The Jack Pearl Show*

Comedy and variety program. Cliff Hall was a regular. Alan Reed participated in a few of the dramatic sketches, but exactly which episodes remains unknown. Sponsored by Lucky Strike Cigarettes. NBC.

November 19, 1933 - April 15, 1934 *The Chase and Sanborn Hour*

Weekly regular: Eddie Cantor. This hour-long program featured a half hour of music and a half hour of variety, which included songs, skits and dramas performed by Cantor and a supporting cast (including Alan Reed). Reed played supporting roles for skits in every broadcast during this season. NBC.

Circa 1934 *The Blubber Bergman Revue*

Weekly quarter-hour program over Chicago's WGN titled Blubber Bergman. In 1937, the program was beamed locally by New York's WNEW and retitled The Blubber Bergman Revue. Among the cast was Alan Reed (for both series), Arlene Francis, Ray Collins and Paul Stewart.

January 3, 1934 - March 14, 1934 *The Sal Hepatica Revue*
Weekly regular: Fred Allen. This half-hour program featured a number of songs and comical skits with a supporting cast that included Alan Reed. NBC. Known Existing Recordings: February 7, 1934 and March 14, 1934

January 3, 1934 - September 26, 1934 *The Jack Pearl Show*
Comedy and variety program. Cliff Hall was a regular. Alan Reed participated in a few of the dramatic sketches, but exactly which episodes remains unknown. Sponsored by Royal Gelatin. NBC.

January 9, 1934 - March 24, 1934 *Saturday Night Party*
Weekly regular: Robert L. Ripley. This hour-long program featured a few songs and a number of trivial and dramatic skits with Alan Reed occasionally supplying a voice-over or performing a supporting role. B.A. Rolfe Orchestra supplied the music. Sponsored by Hudson. NBC.

January 13, 1934 - September 1, 1934 *Al Pearce and His Gang*
Comedian Al Pearce featured a cast of characters referred to as his "gang." During these dates, that included Alan Reed. Blue Network.

March 21, 1934 - July 4, 1934 *The Hour of Smiles*
Weekly regular: Fred Allen. This hour-long program featured a number of songs and comical skits with Alan Reed occasionally playing a supporting role. NBC. Known Existing Recordings: April 4, 1934, April 11, 1934 and April 18, 1934

April 3, 1934 - July 30, 1935 *The Palmolive Beauty Box Theater*
This hour-long program was an anthology of stories ranging from romance to mystery. Features music from the Nat Shilkret Orchestra. Alan Reed played a supporting role in a large number of episodes. Sponsored by Palmolive. NBC. Known Existing Recording: December 25, 1934.

September 3, 1934 - December 26, 1935 *Buck Rogers*
Science-fiction serial starring Curtis Arnall and Adele Ronson. Alan Reed is among the cast of supporting actors. 15-minute series, four-times-a-week. Sponsored by Cocomalt. CBS.

September 3, 1934 - March 29, 1935 *Al Pearce and His Gang*
Comedian Al Pearce featured a cast of characters referred to as his "gang." Alan Reed was among the cast. Two times a week, 15 minutes. Blue Network.

October 1, 1934 - March 27, 1935 *The Shadow*
Weekly regular: Frank Readick (James La Curto replaced Readick for a few weeks beginning November 26, 1934). This half-hour program featured a mystery drama from current issues of Street and Smith's mystery and detective magazines. Alan Reed played a lead or supporting role in most of the broadcasts. Sponsored by D.L.&W. Coal Company. CBS.

Fall of 1934 - Summer of 1935 *The Baker's Broadcast*
Weekly regular: Joe Penner. This half-hour variety program also features Ozzie Nelson, Harriett Hilliard and Feg Murray. Alan Reed appeared on the program on occasion to play a supporting role for a comical or dramatic skit. Sponsored by Fleischmann. Blue Network. Known Existing Recordings: May 5, 1935 and May 11, 1935

October 7, 1934 - November 25, 1934 *The Chase and Sanborn Hour*
Weekly regular: Eddie Cantor. This hour-long program featured a half hour of music and a half hour of variety, which included songs, skits and dramas performed by Cantor and a supporting cast (including Alan Reed). NBC.

July 11, 1934 - June 26, 1935 *Town Hall Tonight*
Weekly regular: Fred Allen. This hour-long program featured a number of songs and comical skits with Alan Reed occasionally playing a supporting role. NBC.

March 8, 1935 - May 3, 1935 *Circus Night in Silvertown*
Weekly regular: Joe Cook, Tim and Irene This 45-minute program featured a number of songs and comical skits with Alan Reed occasionally playing a supporting role. Sponsored by B.F. Goodrich. Blue Network.

March 13, 1935 - May 22, 1935 *Family Hotel*
Comedy and variety program. Cliff Hall and Jack Pearl are regulars. Alan Reed participated in a few of the dramatic sketches, but exactly which episodes remains unknown. Sponsored by Frigidaire. CBS.

April 1, 1935 - September 23, 1935 *The Shadow*
Weekly regular: Frank Readick. This half-hour program featured a mystery drama from current issues of Street and Smith's mystery and detective magazines. Alan Reed played a lead or supporting role in most of the broadcasts. Sponsored by D.L.&W. Coal Company. Mutual Network.

May 13, 1935 - September 27, 1935 *Al Pearce and His Gang*
Comedian Al Pearce featured a cast of characters referred to as his "gang." Alan Reed was among the cast. Three times a week, 15 minutes. NBC.

May 24, 1935 - August 2, 1935 *Circus Night in Silvertown*
Weekly regular: Joe Cook, Tim and Irene. This half-hour program featured a number of songs and comical skits with Alan Reed occasionally playing a supporting role for some of those skits. Sponsored by B.F. Goodrich. NBC. Known Existing Recordings: May 24, 1935 and August. 2, 1935.

August 9, 1935 - December 27, 1935 *The Palmolive Beauty Box Theater*
This hour-long program was an anthology of stories ranging from romance to mystery. Features music from the Al Goodman Orchestra. Alan Reed played a supporting role in a large number of episodes. Sponsored by Palmolive. Blue Network. Known Existing Recording: August 30, 1935.

September 12, 1935 - March 5, 1936 *Harv and Esther*
Alan Reed and Audrey Marsh star in the title roles, a comedy-variety program with fictional names created for the sponsor's benefit. Sponsored by Harvester Cigars. Jack Arthur was the vocalist. CBS.

October 2, 1935 - June 24, 1936 *Town Hall Tonight*
Weekly regular: Fred Allen. This hour-long program featured a number of songs and comical skits with Alan Reed occasionally playing a supporting role. NBC. Known Existing Recordings: October 2, 1935, January 22, 1936, February 26, 1936, April 1, 1936, June 10, 1936 and June 17, 1936.

October 6, 1935 - June 21, 1936 *The Baker's Broadcast*
Weekly regular: Joe Penner. This half-hour variety program also features Ozzie Nelson, Harriett Hilliard and Feg Murray. Alan Reed appeared on the program on occasion in a supporting role. Sponsored by Fleischmann. Blue Network. Known Existing recording: April 12, 1936

October 7, 1935 - March 30, 1936 *Al Pearce and His Gang*
Comedian Al Pearce featured a cast of characters referred to as his "gang." Alan Reed was among the cast. Sponsored by Pepsodent. NBC.

December 30, 1935 - May 22, 1936 *Buck Rogers*
Science-fiction serial starring Matt Crowley and Adele Ronson. Alan Reed is among the cast of supporting actors. Sponsored by Cream of Wheat. Three-times-a-week, 15-minute series. CBS.

January 10, 1936 - April 3, 1936 *Al Pearce and His Gang*
Comedian Al Pearce featured a cast of characters referred to as his "gang." Alan Reed was among the cast. Sponsored by Pepsodent. Blue Network.

January 11, 1936 - February 15, 1936 *The Palmolive Beauty Box Theater*
This hour-long program was an anthology of stories ranging from romance to mystery. Features music from the Al Goodman Orchestra. Alan Reed played a supporting role in a large number of episodes. Sponsored by Palmolive. CBS.

August 6, 1936 - September 28, 1939 *The Royal Gelatin Hour*
Weekly regular: Rudy Vallee. This hour-long program featured musical performances, newly discovered talent, comical skits and a variety of dramas. Alan Reed played a supporting role for a number of the broadcasts. Sponsored by Royal Gelatin. NBC. Known Existing Recordings: a minimum of 63 broadcasts.

September 8, 1936 - August 31, 1937 *True Detective Mysteries*
Anthology series of mystery dramas, sponsored by MacFadden Publications with adaptations from short stories in their magazines. Jack Shuttleworth narrated. Alan Reed was among the cast. Mutual.

September 14, 1936 - circa 1938 *Big Sister*
Serial soap opera about Ruth Evans, a woman who put aside her own happiness for the sake of her younger, orphaned siblings. Alice Frost stars as Ruth Evans. Alan Reed was among the cast during the first two years. Exact dates of Reed's appearance or the character(s) he played remain unknown. 15 minutes, five-days-a-week. Sponsored by Lever Brothers. CBS.

September 23, 1936 - June 30, 1937 *Town Hall Tonight*
Weekly regular: Fred Allen. This hour-long program featured a number of songs and comical skits with Alan Reed occasionally playing a supporting role. NBC. Known Existing Recordings: September 23, 1936, September 30, 1936, October 7, 1936, October 14, 1936, October 28, 1936, November 4, 1936, December 16, 1936, January 27, 1937, March 10, 1937 and March 17, 1937.

October 4, 1936 - June 27, 1937 *The Baker's Broadcast*
Weekly regular: Feg Murray. This half-hour variety program also features the music of Ozzie Nelson and Harriett Hilliard. Alan Reed appeared on the program on occasion to play a supporting role for a comical or dramatic skit. Sponsored by Fleischmann. Blue Network.

October 17, 1936 - October 10, 1937 *Saturday Night Party*
Weekly regulars: Jane Pickens and Walter O'Keefe. This hour-long show combined music and dramatic skits. Alan Reed occasionally played a supporting role. Sponsored by Sealtest. NBC.

November 9, 1936 - June 25, 1937 *The Jack Pearl Show*
Comedy and variety program. Cliff Hall was a regular. Alan Reed participated in a few of the dramatic sketches, but exactly which episodes remains unknown. Tommy Dorsey supplied some of the music. Sponsored by Raleigh and Kool Cigarettes. NBC.

January 2, 1937 - June 26, 1937 *Shell Chateau*
Weekly regular: Joe Cook. This hour-long program featured a number of songs and comical skits with Alan Reed occasionally playing a supporting role. Sponsored by Shell Oil. NBC.

January 4, 1937 - December 31, 1937 *Myrt and Marge*
(also known as *The Story of Myrt and Marge*) Soap opera about a seasoned chorus girl and her crime-fighting husband, a district attorney. Myrtle Vail, Vinton Hayworth and Donna Damerel were regulars. Alan Reed, Santos Ortega and Ed Begley were among the actors playing a number of recurring characters. Five-times-a-week, 15 minutes. Sponsored by Super Suds. CBS.

January 13, 1937 - October 6, 1937 *The Palmolive Beauty Box Theater*
This half-hour program was an anthology of stories ranging from romance to mystery. Features music from the Al Goodman Orchestra. Jessica Dragonette was a weekly singer. Alan Reed played a supporting role in a large number of episodes. Sponsored by Palmolive. CBS. Known Existing Recording: January 27, February 3, February 10, April 14, April 21, April 28, May 12, May 19, May 26, June 2, June 9, June 30, July 14, July 28, Aug. 11, September 1, September 8, September 15 and September 29, 1937

July 16, 1937 - October 1, 1937 *Believe It or Not*
Weekly regular: Robert L. Ripley. This half-hour program featured a couple songs and trivial and dramatic skits. Alan Reed frequently played a supporting role for some of those skits. Sponsored by General Foods (often Post Bran Flakes). NBC.

September 26, 1937 - March 20, 1938 *The Shadow*
Weekly regulars: Orson Welles and Agnes Moorehead. Dramatic mystery program featuring a crime fighter with the ability to become invisible. Alan Reed was among a group of radio actors who frequently played supporting roles in many of the episodes. Exact broadcasts remain unknown. Radio Guide (a 1939 issue) credits Alan Reed as one of the "clear and resonant voices" on the program. Sponsored by Blue Coal. Mutual Network.

October 3, 1937 - June 26, 1938 *The Baker's Broadcast*
Weekly regular: Feg Murray. This half-hour variety program also features the music of Ozzie Nelson and Harriett Hilliard. Alan Reed appeared on the program on occasion to play a supporting role. Sponsored by Fleischmann. Blue Network. Known Existing Recordings: November 7, 1937

October 9, 1937 - April 16, 1938 *Believe It or Not*
Weekly regular: Robert L. Ripley. This half-hour program featured a few songs and trivial and dramatic skits. Alan Reed frequently played a supporting role for some of those skits. Sponsored by General Foods. NBC.

November 17, 1937 - June 29, 1938 *Town Hall Tonight*
Weekly regular: Fred Allen. This hour-long program featured a number of songs and comical skits with Alan Reed occasionally playing a supporting role. NBC. Known Existing Recordings: December 22, 1937, December 29, 1937, March 23, 1938, May 18, 1938, May 25, 1938, June 1, 1938, June 8, 1938, June 22, 1938, and June 29, 1938.

1938 Syndication *The Shadow*
Weekly regulars: Orson Welles and Agnes Moorehead. Dramatic mystery program featuring a crime fighter with the ability to become invisible. Alan Reed was among a group of radio actors who frequently played supporting roles in many of the episodes. Exact broadcasts remain unknown. A total of 26 episodes were recorded and syndicated, broadcast at various times over various radio stations across the country. Sponsored by B.F. Goodrich.

January 3, 1938 - March 27, 1942 *Myrt and Marge*
(also known as *The Story of Myrt and Marge*) Soap opera about a seasoned chorus girl and her crime-fighting husband, a district attorney. Myrtle Vail, Vinton Hayworth and Donna Damerel were regulars. Alan Reed, Santos Ortega and Ed Begley were among the actors playing a number of recurring characters. Five-times-a-week, 15 minutes. Sponsored by Super Suds. CBS.

February 26, 1938 - May 7, 1938 *Great Plays*
This hour-long program ran a total of 11 broadcasts. Alan Reed was a supporting player for three of these episodes, and most likely more: "The Great Magician" (March 12), "A Midsummer Night's Dream" (March 26, 1938), and "The School for Scandal" (April 16, 1938). Blue Network.

March 7, 1938 - May 27, 1938 *Valiant Lady*
Soap opera starring Joan Blaine in the title role. Alan Reed played both villain (Mr. Wright) and friend (Mike Hagen) in the same 1938 storyline that began and concluded on these dates. The series was heard on various runs till 1952, but this was the only known storyline to include Alan Reed in the cast. Sponsored by General Mills for Gold Medal Flour. 15-minute series, five-days-a-week. CBS.

March 11, 1938 - September 2, 1938 *The Royal Crown Revue*
(also known as the *Tim and Irene* program) Vaudeville-style comedy program. Fredda Gibson, Charlie Cantor and Alan Reed were among the weekly cast of regulars. Sponsored by Nehi Soft Drinks. Blue Network.

March 27, 1939 - October 6, 1939 *Myrt and Marge*
(also known as *The Story of Myrt and Marge*) Soap opera about a seasoned chorus girl and her crime-fighting husband, a district attorney. Myrtle Vail, Vinton Hayworth and Donna Damerel were regulars. Alan Reed, Santos Ortega and Ed Begley were among the actors playing a number of recurring characters. Five-times-a-week, 15 minutes. Sponsored by Super Suds. Mutual.

April 5, 1938 - March 28, 1939 *True Detective Mysteries*
Anthology series of mystery dramas, with adaptations of short stories from
MacFadden Publications. Jack Shuttleworth narrated. Alan Reed was among
the cast. Beginning in January 1939, the program went from 30 minutes to
15 minutes in length. Sponsored by Listerine. Mutual.

April 26, 1938 - July 26, 1938 *Believe It or Not*
Weekly regular: Robert L. Ripley. This half-hour program featured a few songs
and trivial and dramatic skits. Alan Reed frequently played a supporting role
for some of those skits. Sponsored by General Foods. NBC.

June 2, 1938 - August 25, 1938 *Pulitzer Prize Plays*
This half-hour program featured dramas that had won the Pulitzer Prize.
Alan Reed played a supporting role in at least three of these broadcasts. "They
Knew What They Wanted" (August 11) and "Strange Interlude: Parts 1 and
2" (August 18 and 25). Milton Cross was the announcer. Blue Network.

August 8, 1938 - October 3, 1938 *Believe It or Not*
Weekly regular: Robert L. Ripley. This half-hour program featured a few songs
and trivial and dramatic skits. Alan Reed frequently played a supporting role.
Sponsored by General Foods. NBC. Known Existing Episodes: November
26, 1937 and May 24, 1938.

September 25, 1938 - March 19, 1939 *The Shadow*
Weekly regulars: Bill Johnstone and Agnes Moorehead. Dramatic mystery program featuring a crime fighter with the ability to become invisible. Alan Reed
was among a group of radio actors who frequently played supporting roles.
Sponsored by Blue Coal. Mutual Network.

October 5, 1938 - June 28, 1939 *Town Hall Tonight*
Weekly regular: Fred Allen. This hour-long program featured a number of
songs and comical skits with Alan Reed occasionally playing a supporting
role for some of those skits. NBC. Known Existing Recordings: December
21, 1938, January 25, 1939, February 8, 1939, February 22, 1939, March 22,
1939, April 5, 1939 and June 21, 1939.

October 16, 1938 - May 7, 1939 *Great Plays*
This hour-long program ran a total of 29 broadcasts. Alan Reed was a supporting
player for six of these episodes, and most likely more: "Everyman" (October 23,
1938), "The Great Magician" (October 30, 1938), "A Midsummer Night's Dream"
(November 13, 1938), "Le Cid" (December 4, 1938), "The School for Scandal"
(January 15, 1939), and "The Blue Bird" (April 2, 1939). For some of these he
was reprising his roles from the previous run in spring of 1938. Blue Network.

Circa 1939 *Pipe Dreams*
Comedy series starring Alan Reed. 5-minute program broadcast over NBC.

1939 Syndication *The Amazing Interplanetary Adventures of Flash Gordon*
15-minute series, syndicated across the country. Exact dates vary by location. Local sponsors varied from station to station. Cast included Maurice Franklin, Franc Hale and Alan Reed.

1939 Syndication *The Shadow*
Weekly regulars: Bill Johnstone and Marjorie Anderson. Dramatic mystery program featuring a crime fighter with the ability to become invisible. Alan Reed was among a group of radio actors who frequently played supporting roles. Exact broadcasts remain unknown. A total of 25 episodes were recorded and syndicated, broadcast at various times over various radio stations across the country. Sponsored by B.F. Goodrich.

March 24, 1939 *The Campbell Playhouse*
Weekly regular: Orson Welles. This hour-long anthology featured a variety of dramas, with Welles either in the lead or a supporting role. Each week a female actress of Hollywood or Broadway would assume the female lead. Alan Reed played a supporting role in this dramatization of Twentieth Century, the Ben Hecht and Charles MacArthur stage play. Sponsored by Campbell Soups. CBS.

May 19, 1939 - October 10, 1939 *Breezin' Along*
Musical variety program with the Johnny Green Orchestra. Jack Smith and Beverly Freeland were co-hosts. Alan Reed later replaced Smith as co-host. Sponsored by Philip Morris. Mutual Network.

September 24, 1939 - April 7, 1940 *The Shadow*
Weekly regulars: Bill Johnstone and Marjorie Anderson
Dramatic mystery program featuring a crime fighter with the ability to become invisible. Alan Reed was among a group of radio actors who frequently played supporting roles. Sponsored by Blue Coal. Mutual Network.

October 4, 1939 - June 26, 1940 *The Fred Allen Show*
Weekly regular: Fred Allen. This hour-long series featured a variety of comedy and music, mostly comedy. Alan Reed appeared almost weekly in supporting roles for some of the comedy skits. Sponsored by Ipana-Sal Hepatica. NBC.

October 15, 1939 - May 5, 1940 *Great Plays*
This hour-long program ran a total of 29 broadcasts. Alan Reed was a supporting performer for a number of episodes. Exact broadcasts remain unknown. Blue Network.

October 20, 1939 - April 12, 1940 *Quixie-Doodles*
Weekly regular: Colonel Stoopnagle. Radio quiz of satirical nonsense. Colonel Stoopnagle often asked silly questions on the program, and tried to see if the weekend guest could figure the answers. Prize money was awarded. Alan Reed was the announcer. Sponsored by Mennen. Mutual Network.

November 8, 1939 - May 1, 1940 *Breezin' Along*
Musical variety program with the Johnny Green Orchestra. Alan Reed and Beverly Freeland were co-hosts. Title of program changed to Jingo as of April 17, 1940. Sponsored by Philip Morris. Blue Network.

May 5, 1940 - July 28, 1940 *Jingo*
Musical variety program with the Johnny Green Orchestra. Alan Reed and Beverly Freeland were co-hosts. Sponsored by Philip Morris. CBS.

July 24, 1940 - September 1, 1943 *Manhattan at Midnight*
Romantic serial drama with Jeanette Nolan, Alan Reed and Ted de Corsia in the leads. Sponsored by Energine and Sterling Drugs. Blue Network.

September 15, 1940 *The Aldrich Family*
Situation comedy. Ezra Stone plays the lead of Henry Aldrich. Sponsored by Jell-O. NBC.

September 29, 1940 - April 20, 1941 *The Shadow*
Weekly regulars: Bill Johnstone and Marjorie Anderson. Dramatic mystery program featuring a crime fighter with the ability to become invisible. Alan Reed was among a group of radio actors who frequently played supporting roles in many of the episodes. Sponsored by Blue Coal. Mutual Network.

September 29, 1940 - March 23, 1941 *Quixie-Doodles*
Weekly regular: Colonel Stoopnagle. Radio quiz of satirical nonsense. Colonel Stoopnagle often asked silly questions on the program, and tried to see if the weekend guest could figure the answers. Prize money was awarded. Alan Reed was the announcer. Sponsored by Mennen. CBS Network.

October 2, 1940 - June 25, 1941 *The Texaco Star Theater*
Weekly regular: Fred Allen. This hour-long series featured a variety of comedy and music, mostly comedy. Alan Reed appeared almost weekly in supporting roles for some of the comedy skits. Sponsored by Texaco. CBS.

October 13, 1940 - May 4, 1941 *Great Plays*
This hour-long program ran a total of 29 broadcasts. Alan Reed was a supporting performer for a number of episodes. Exact broadcasts remain unknown. Blue Network.

December 30, 1940 *The Lux Radio Theatre*
"A Little Bit of Heaven" with Gloria Jean, C. Aubrey Smith, Frank Albertson and Alan Reed in the cast. An adaptation of the classic Universal Studios film; hosted by Cecil B. DeMille. Sponsored by Lux. CBS.

March 21, 1941 - August 8, 1941 *Great Moments From Great Plays*
Anthology series featuring adaptations of stage plays. Ray Bloch supplied the music. Alan Reed played supporting roles for a few of the episodes, and a co-starring role (with Frank Readick) in an adaptation of Steinbeck's Of Mice and Men on May 16, 1941. Sponsored by Philip Morris. CBS.

July 2, 1941 - September 24, 1941 *The Treasury Hour*
Patriotic WWII series with different stars each week entertaining radio listeners while attempting to convince them to buy war bonds. Alan Reed appears in the July 30, 1941 broadcast reading Herman Wouk's The Ballad of the Letherneck Corps. It is possible that he made an appearance in another episode during the series. The hour-long episodes were broadcast over the CBS Network.

September 28, 1941 - March 22, 1942 *The Shadow*
Weekly regulars: Bill Johnstone and Marjorie Anderson. Dramatic mystery program featuring a crime fighter with the ability to become invisible. Alan Reed was among a group of radio actors who frequently played supporting roles in many of the episodes. Sponsored by Blue Coal. Mutual Network.

September 30, 1941 - December 23, 1941 *Millions for Defense*
Patriotic WWII series with different stars each week entertaining radio listeners while attempting to convince them to buy war bonds. Alan Reed appears in at least two of the episodes (and possibly more). On October 28, Reed played a supporting role in the D.H. Johnson drama *The Last Boat* with performers Fay Wray and John Beal. On November 26, Reed played a supporting role in Mark Hellinger's play, *His Word* as a Soldier. Sponsored by Bendix Aviation. Blue Network.

October 1, 1941 - February 25, 1942 *The Texaco Star Theater*
Weekly regular: Fred Allen. This series featured a variety of comedy and music, mostly comedy. Alan Reed appeared almost weekly in supporting roles for some of the skits. Sponsored by Texaco. CBS.

October 21, 1941 *We, The People*
A singular mix of humor, pathos, tragedy, sentiment and Hollywood glamour Alan Reed plays a supporting role for a segment in this episode. Sponsored by Sanka. CBS.

November 16, 1941 - August 30, 1942 *Famous Fireside Plays*
This hour-long program ran a total of 42 broadcasts. Alan Reed was a supporting performer for a number of episodes. Exact broadcasts remain unknown. Thism series is also recognized as part of the Great Plays radio series. Blue Network.

January 24, 1942 - September 2, 1944 *Abie's Irish Rose*
Weekly radio drama based on the Broadway hit of the same name. Story tells of Abie and Rosemary Levy, a young married couple from Jewish and Catholic families. Alan Reed plays the recurring role of one of the two feuding fathers. Sponsored by Drene. NBC.

March 8, 1942 - June 28, 1942 *The Texaco Star Theater*
Weekly regular: Fred Allen. This series featured a variety of comedy and music, mostly comedy. Alan Reed appeared almost weekly in supporting roles for some of the skits. Sponsored by Texaco. CBS.

March 17, 1942 - June 30, 1942 *Duffy's Tavern*
Weekly regular: Ed Gardner. Situation comedy about the mishaps in a New York City tavern. Alan Reed plays the recurring role of Clancy the cop. Sponsored by Sanka. CBS.

August 31, 1942 *The Columbia Workshop*
Alan Reed co-stars with Minerva Pious, Art Carney and Jim Backus in a series of slapstick skits titled "All Out for Comedy."

September 27, 1942 - March 21, 1943 *The Shadow*
Weekly regulars: Bill Johnstone and Marjorie Anderson. Dramatic mystery program featuring a crime fighter with the ability to become invisible. Alan Reed was among a group of radio actors who frequently played supporting roles in many of the episodes. Sponsored by Blue Coal. Mutual Network.

October 4, 1942 - June 27, 1943 *The Texaco Star Theater*
Weekly regular: Fred Allen. This half-hour series featured a variety of comedy and music, mostly comedy. Alan Reed appeared almost weekly in supporting roles for some of the comedy skits. Sponsored by Texaco. CBS.

October 6, 1942 - June 29, 1943 *Duffy's Tavern*
Weekly regular: Ed Gardner. Situation comedy about the mishaps in a New York City tavern. Alan Reed plays the recurring role of Clancy the cop. Sponsored by Ipana. Blue Network.

December 13, 1942 *The Grape-Nuts Program*
Weekly regular: Jack Benny. Benny and guest Gary Cooper decide to wander the streets of New York City. Alan Reed plays a supporting role. Sponsored by Grape Nuts. NBC.

July 1, 1943 *The Kraft Music Hall*
Weekly regular: Bing Crosby. Musical variety program. Alan Reed appears as "Falstaff Openshaw" and recites a war poem. Sponsored by Kraft. NBC.

December 12, 1943 - June 25, 1944 *The Texaco Star Theater*
Weekly regular: Fred Allen. This half-hour series featured a variety of comedy and music, mostly comedy. Alan Reed appeared weekly in supporting roles for all of the comedy skits. Sponsored by Texaco. CBS.

October 5, 1943 - June 27, 1944 *Duffy's Tavern*
Weekly regular: Ed Gardner. Situation comedy about the mishaps in a New York City tavern. Alan Reed plays the recurring role of Clancy the cop. Sponsored by Ipana. Blue Network.

November 25, 1943 *The Elgin Company's Second Annual Tribute To The Armed Forces*
A two-hour all-star WWII special featuring a variety of songs and skits. Guests include George Burns and Gracie Allen, Frances Langford, Edgar Bergen, Ginny Simms, Ed Gardner, and Alan Reed as "Falstaff Openshaw," who recites a poem titled "Downfall." Sponsored by Elgin Watches. CBS.

February 5, 1944 *The Grantland Rice Story*
(also known as The Sportsmen's Club) Alan Reed plays a supporting role in a drama titled, "Second Wind." Also in the cast: Sam Wanamaker. NBC.

March 30, 1944 *The Abbott and Costello Show*
Weekly regulars: Bud Abbott and Lou Costello. Alan Ladd is the guest celebrity. Alan Reed participates in a skit about a radio soap opera. Sponsored by Camel Cigarettes. NBC.

June 12, 1944 - December 8, 1944 *Johnny Mercer Music Shop*
Weekly regular: Jo Stafford. Broadcast five times a week for fifteen minutes, this musical variety series featured Alan Reed as Falstaff Openshaw for an unknown number of episodes. Sponsored by Chesterfield Cigarettes. NBC.

September 15, 1944 - June 8, 1945 *Duffy's Tavern*
Weekly regular: Ed Gardner. Situation comedy about the mishaps in a New York City tavern. Alan Reed plays the recurring role of Clancy the cop. Sponsored by Ipana. NBC.

September 17, 1944 - June 10, 1945 *Post Toasties Time*
Weekly regular: Fanny Brice. Situation comedy about a young girl named Baby Snooks who got into trouble and required her father to bail her out. Alan Reed reportedly played the recurring role of Daddy's boss, Mr. Weemish. He also played the role of "Daddy" when the show was produced in New York. Sponsored by Post Toasties. CBS.

October 19, 1944 *The Kraft Music Hall*
Weekly regular: George Murphy. Musical variety program. Alan Reed appears briefly. Sponsored by Kraft. NBC.

October 29, 1944 *The Lucky Strike Program*
Weekly regular: Jack Benny. Alan Reed appears as "Falstaff Openshaw." Sponsored by Lucky Strike. NBC.

December 23, 1944 *The Sportsmen's Club*
(formerly known as *The Grantland Rice Story*) Alan Reed reprises his February 1944 supporting role in the drama titled "Second Wind." Also in the cast: Sam Wanamaker. NBC.

1945 - 1946 Syndication *Easy Aces*
Produced by ZIV, this syndicated show was produced and broadcast throughout the mid-forties. Alan Reed played a recurring role in a number of broadcasts. Each episode ran fifteen minutes long. Anacin was the sponsor for a number of broadcasts.

February 25, 1945 *The Philco Radio Hall of Fame*
Variety series featuring music, comedy and drama with a weekly rotating cast of celebrities from Hollywood and Broadway. Ed Gardner and the cast of Duffy's Tavern perform a skit in which Alan Reed reprises his role of Clancy the Cop.

September 16, 1945 - June 9, 1946 *The Baby Snooks Show*
Weekly regular: Fanny Brice. Situation comedy about a young girl named Baby Snooks who got into trouble and required her father to bail her out. Alan Reed played the recurring role of Daddy's boss, Mr. Weemish. Sponsored by Sanka. CBS.

September 21, 1945 - June 14, 1946 *Duffy's Tavern*
Weekly regular: Ed Gardner. Situation comedy about the mishaps in a New York City tavern. Alan Reed plays the recurring role of Clancy the cop. Sponsored by Ipana. NBC. *Note: An excerpt from at least two broadcasts were later featured in an AFRS broadcast of* To the Rear March. *The excerpt featured Alan Reed in the cast.*

October 4, 1945 *Command Performance*
The date listed is the recording date, not broadcast date. This radio program was syndicated, so the broadcast dates vary from station to station. Alan Reed appears as "Falstaff Openshaw" to read another one of his poems.

October 7, 1945 - June 30, 1946 *The Fred Allen Show*
Weekly regular: Fred Allen. This half-hour series featured a variety of comedy and music, mostly comedy. Alan Reed appeared almost weekly in supporting roles for some of the skits. It is possible that Reed signed on to play supporting roles beginning with the broadcast of January 6, 1946. From January 6 to June 23, he appeared in 15 broadcasts, but there are no known credits from October to December 1945. Sponsored by Tenderleaf Tea. NBC. *Note: An excerpt from at least two broadcasts were later featured in an AFRS broadcast of* To the Rear March. *The excerpt featured Alan Reed in the cast.*

October 17, 1945 *Time to Smile*
(also known as *The Eddie Cantor Show*) *Weekly regular: Eddie Cantor.* When Eddie finds himself fired from the job, and tries to convince the sponsor to give him his job back. Alan Reed plays the role of Mr. Moran, the sponsor. Don Wilson is also among the cast. Sponsored by Trushay. NBC.

October 24, 1945 *The Jack Carson Show*
Arthur Treacher and Alan Reed are among the cast. Sponsored by Campbell
Soups. CBS. *Note: An excerpt from this broadcast was later featured in an AFRS
broadcast of* To the Rear March. *The excerpt featured Alan Reed in the cast.*

October 29, 1945 *The Cavalcade Of America*
Guest Humphrey Bogart stars in the story, "My Son, John," about a jinxed
submarine. Jerry Hausner and Alan Reed are among the supporting cast.
Sponsored by DuPont. NBC.

December 25, 1945 *The Elgin Christmas Day Greeting To America*
Two-hour holiday special with Allan Jones, Bob Hope, Jack Benny, Red Skelton, Don Ameche, Ginny Simms, Larry Storch and Alan Reed. Sponsored
by Elgin Watches. CBS.

June 30, 1946 *Command Performance*
(This is the show's recording date, not the date of broadcast.) Janet Blair is guest
emcee. Danny Kaye, Carmen Miranda, Hal Kanter and Alan Reed are in
the cast.

July 7, 1946 *The Eternal Light*
"The Wise Men of Chelm" is a spiritual drama with Leon Janney, Edgar Stehli,
Guy Repp, Norman Rose and Alan Reed in the cast. NBC.

September 3, 1946 - June 24, 1947 *Mr. Blanc's Fix-It-Shop*
(also known as *The Mel Blanc Show*) Situation comedy with Mel Blanc playing
himself, an addled young man who runs a repair business called The Fix-It-
Shop. Alan Reed played the recurring role of Mr. Potchnik, the piano teacher.
The series ran a total of 41 broadcasts. Reed appeared in at least 10 of those
broadcasts. Sponsored by Colgate. CBS.

September 6, 1946 - May 30, 1947 *The Baby Snooks Show*
Weekly regular: Fanny Brice. Situation comedy about a young girl named Baby
Snooks who got into trouble and required her father to bail her out. Alan
Reed played the recurring role of Daddy's boss, Mr. Weemish. Sponsored
by Jell-O. CBS.

September 7, 1946 - July 5, 1947 *The Life of Riley*
Situation comedy with William Bendix as Chester A. Riley. Alan Reed played
a number of supporting roles on the series. The program premiered on April
26, 1941, but Reed's earliest known appearance on the program is June 7, 1947.
He appeared on the program a large number of times after June 7. Sponsor
was Teel Dentifrice until January 11, 1947 when Dreft took over. NBC.

September 20, 1946 – May 30, 1947 *The Alan Young Show*
Weekly regular: Alan Young. Comedy variety series. Guest Art Linkletter invites Alan to join his People Are Funny radio program. Supporting cast includes Veola Vonn, Jim Backus, Charles Cantor and Alan Reed. It remains unclear exactly how many episodes Reed appeared on, but the broadcast of December 13, 1946 has been confirmed. Sponsored by Ipana. NBC.

October 2, 1946 - June 25, 1947 *Duffy's Tavern*
Weekly regular: Ed Gardner. Situation comedy about the mishaps in a New York City tavern. Alan Reed plays the recurring role of Clancy the cop. Sponsored by Ipana. NBC.

October 2, 1946 - June 25, 1947 *The Jack Carson Show*
Weekly regular: Jack Carson. Musical variety program. Alan Reed played supporting roles in a number of episodes. Episodes confirmed to feature Reed in the cast: December 18, 1946, January 22, 1947 and April 9, 1947. Sponsored by Campbell Soups

October 8, 1946 *Cresta Blanca Hollywood Players*
"Golden Boy." Story about a boxer who loves to play the violin. Cast members include John Garfield, Lynn Bari, Gerald Mohr and Alan Reed. Sponsored by Cresta Blanca Wines. CBS.

December 9, 1946 *The Lux Radio Theatre*
"Together Again" with Irene Dunne, Walter Pidgeon, Lillian Randolph and Alan Reed in the cast. An adaptation of the classic Columbia film from 1944. Host is William Keighley. Sponsored by Lux. CBS.

December 16, 1946 *The Lux Radio Theatre*
"Killer Kates" with Jack Benny, Gail Patrick, Gale Gordon, Norman Field and Alan Reed in the cast. This drama was based on an unproduced Warner Bros. Story "The Man They Couldn't Kill." Host is William Keighley. Sponsored by Lux. CBS.

January 27, 1947 *The Lux Radio Theatre*
"Cluny Brown" with Charles Boyer, Olivia deHavilland, Gale Gordon and Alan Reed in the cast. An adaptation of the 20th Century Fox movie. Host is William Keighley. Sponsored by Lux. CBS.

February 10, 1947 *The Lux Radio Theatre*
"Frenchman's Creek" with Joan Fontaine, Gerald Mohr, David Niven and Alan Reed in the cast. An adaptation of the classic 1944 Paramount Studios film. Host is William Keighley. Sponsored by Lux. CBS.

February 17, 1947 *The Lux Radio Theatre*
"Devotion" with Jane Wyman, Virginia Bruce, Vincent Price, Norman Field and Alan Reed in the cast. An adaptation of the classic 1946 Warner Bros. film. Host is William Keighley. Sponsored by Lux. CBS.

February 24, 1947 *The Lux Radio Theatre*
"Kitty" with Paulette Goddard, Patric Knowles, Raymond Lawrence and Alan Reed in the cast. An adaptation of the classic 1946 Paramount Pictures film. Host is William Keighley. Sponsored by Lux. CBS.

March 3, 1947 *The Whistler*
"The Blue Legend." A schemer/con artist manages to get a piece of the action on a valuable Alaskan gold mine, and resorts to murder. Cast includes Virginia Gregg and Alan Reed. Sponsored by Signal Oil. CBS.

March 17, 1947 *The Lux Radio Theatre*
"Leave Her to Heaven" with Cornell Wilde, Gene Tierney, Kay Christopher and Alan Reed in the cast. An adaptation of the classic 20th Century Fox film. Host is William Keighley. Sponsored by Lux. CBS.

March 21, 1947 - December 13, 1947 *Leave It To Bill*
(also known as *The Bill Goodwin Show*) Goodwin plays the role of a "hotshot insurance salesman." Peggy Kudsen played the role of his girlfriend Phillipa. Alan Reed played a supporting role in a number of episodes. Episodes confirmed to have Reed in the cast: March 21, 1947 and May 17, 1947.

April 1947 *Here's To Veterans*
Episode #47. Syndicated program. This 15-minute episode features a few minutes from a previously broadcast Baby Snooks episode with Alan Reed as Mr. Blair, Daddy's boss.

April 11, 1947 - June 20, 1947 *My Friend Irma*
Situation comedy starring Marie Wilson as Irma Peterson, a stenographer by trade, who often got into trouble. Her boss, Mr. Clyde, was played by Alan Reed in most of the episodes. Sponsored by Pepsodent. CBS.

April 17, 1947 *Suspense*
"The Green-Eyed Monster." A man retrieves his stolen car, only to find the dead body of his wife stashed in the trunk. Guest stars Lloyd Nolan. Supporting cast includes Cathy Lewis and Alan Reed. Sponsored by Roma Wines. CBS.

May 2, 1947 *This Is Your FBI*
"The Henpecked Swindler." Dean Carlton is the narrator. Alan Reed is among the supporting cast. Sponsored by the Equitable Life Assurance Company. ABC.

June 30, 1947 - July 28, 1947 *My Friend Irma*
Situation comedy starring Marie Wilson as Irma Peterson, a stenographer by trade, who often got into trouble. Her boss, Mr. Clyde, was played by Alan Reed in most of the episodes. Sponsored by Pepsodent. CBS.

July 24, 1947 *The Man Called X*
"Destination: Manila." International Intrigue series about a shipment of radium on a cross-country flight. Herbert Marshall stars; Leon Belasco and Alan Reed are in the supporting cast. Sponsored by Frigidaire. CBS.

August 4, 1947 - June 27, 1949 *My Friend Irma*
Situation comedy starring Marie Wilson as Irma Peterson, a stenographer by trade, who often got into trouble. Her boss, Mr. Clyde, was played by Alan Reed in most of the episodes. Sponsored by Pepsodent. CBS.

September 5, 1947 - May 28, 1948 *The Baby Snooks Show*
Weekly regular: Fanny Brice. Situation comedy about a young girl named Baby Snooks who got into trouble and required her father to bail her out. Alan Reed played the recurring role of Daddy's boss, Mr. Weemish. Sponsored by Jell-O. CBS.

September 6, 1947 - June 26, 1948 *The Life of Riley*
Situation comedy with William Bendix as Chester A. Riley. Alan Reed played a number of supporting roles on the series. Sponsored by Dreft. NBC.

September 8, 1947 *The Cavalcade Of America*
"Kitchen Scientist." Biography of Fanny Farmer, a woman who revolutionized the way home cooking was accomplished. Cast included Ida Lupino, Janet Scott and Alan Reed. Sponsored by DuPont. NBC.

September 21, 1947 *The Chase and Sanborn Program*
Weekly regular: Edgar Bergen and Charlie McCarthy. Guests Donald Duck (Ogden Nash) and Walt Disney assist in a drama titled, "Jack and the Beanstalk" with Alan Reed in the supporting cast. This episode originated from Pasadena, California. Sponsored by Chase and Sanborn Coffee. NBC.

September 22, 1947 *The Cavalcade Of America*
"The Girl Who Ran for President." Biography of Belva Lockwood, who fought for equal rights for women and ran against Grover Cleveland. Cast included Virginia Bruce and Alan Reed. Sponsored by DuPont. NBC.

September 28, 1947 *The Chase and Sanborn Program*
Weekly regular: Edgar Bergen and Charlie McCarthy. Guest Betty Hutton romances Charlie McCarthy. This episode originated from Santa Monica, California. Sponsored by Chase and Sanborn Coffee. NBC.

September 29, 1947 *The Cavalcade Of America*
"Big Boy." Biography of Babe Ruth. Cast included Brian Donlevy and Alan Reed. Sponsored by DuPont. NBC.

October 1, 1947 - June 23, 1948 *Duffy's Tavern*
Weekly regular: Ed Gardner. Situation comedy about the mishaps in a New York City tavern. Alan Reed plays the weekly role of Clancy the cop. In previous seasons, he played the recurring role. Beginning with this season, he played the role on a regular weekly basis. Sponsored by Ipana. NBC.

October 2, 1947 *The Voyage Of The Scarlet Queen*
"The Fat Trader and the Sword of Apokejam." High adventure on the high seas. Cast includes Elliott Reid, Ben Wright and Alan Reed. Mutual Network.

October 5, 1947 - July 1, 1949 *The Ford Theater*
Hour-long anthology program. A total of 79 episodes were broadcast. According to one reference guide, Alan Reed played a supporting role for at least one episode, but the exact title and broadcast date remain elusive. NBC and CBS.

October 13, 1947 *The Cavalcade Of America*
"The Forge." Biography of Elphalet Remington and how he went into the firearms business. Cast included Ronald Reagan, Barbara Fuller and Alan Reed. Sponsored by DuPont. NBC.

October 27, 1947 *The Lux Radio Theatre*
"Stairway to Heaven" with Nigel Bruce, Ray Milland, Ann Blyth, Ben Wright and Alan Reed in the cast. An adaptation of the classic 1947 film. Host is William Keighley. Sponsored by Lux. CBS.

November 1, 1947 *Smilin' Ed McConnell's Buster Brown Gang*
Children's program with Alan Reed among the supporting cast. Sponsored by Buster Brown Shows. NBC.

November 16, 1947 *The Man Called X*
Script remains untitled. A large quantity of a rare drug has disappeared en route to Greece. Starring Herbert Marshall. Supporting cast includes Leon Belasco, Cathy Lewis and Alan Reed. Sponsored by Frigidaire. CBS.

December 4, 1947 *The Young At Heart*
Audition (pilot) episode for a proposed radio program that never made it to the airwaves. The date listed is the date of recording, not the broadcast. Intended as a children's program. Drama for this pilot was "Treasure Island." Cast includes Jerry Farber, Marvin Miller, Harry Lang and Alan Reed.

December 8, 1947 *The Lux Radio Theatre*
"Ride the Pink Horse" with Robert Montgomery, Wanda Hendrix, Thomas Gomez and Alan Reed in the cast. An adaptation of the classic 1947 film by Ben Hecht and Charles Lederer. Host is William Keighley. Sponsored by Lux. CBS.

December 22, 1947 *The Lux Radio Theatre*
"Miracle on 34th Street" with Maureen O'Hara, Edmund Gwenn, John Payne, Natalie Wood and Alan Reed in the cast. Host is William Keighley. Sponsored by Lux. CBS.

December 24, 1947 *The Abbott and Costello Show*
Weekly regular: Bud Abbott and Lou Costello. Lou Costello meets Santa Claus and tells a holiday story to the children. Alan Reed plays the role of Santa. ABC.

1948 - 1950 Syndication *Box 13*
Syndicated series that premiered over WOR in New York on August 22, 1948. The exact dates and times varied by stations across the country. A total of 52 episodes were created. Produced by Alan Ladd's Mayfair Productions. Ladd starred as Dan Holiday, a fiction writer retired from the newspaper game, who seeks out mystery and adventure. Alan Reed played a supporting role in a number of episodes.

January 12, 1948 *The Lux Radio Theatre*
"Kiss of Death" with Victor Mature, Coleen Gray, Richard Widmark and Alan Reed in the cast. An adaptation of the Ben Hecht and Charles Lederer screenplay of the same name. Host is William Keighley. Sponsored by Lux. CBS.

January 24, 1948 *Suspense*
"The Black Angel" and "Eve." (This episode actually has two separate titles.) When a Hollywood producer is framed for murder, his actress-wife gets into the act. Cast includes June Havoc, Lurene Tuttle and Alan Reed. CBS.

February 18, 1948 *The Jimmy Durante Show*
Weekly regular: Jimmy Durante. Alan Reed is in the supporting cast. Sponsored by Rexall. NBC.

February 23, 1948 *The Lux Radio Theatre*
"T-Men" with Dennis O'Keefe, Gail Patrick, Gerald Mohr, Tony Barrett and Alan Reed in the cast. An adaptation of the 1947 Eagle-Lion film. Host is William Keighley. Sponsored by Lux. CBS.

March 8, 1948 *The Clock*
"The Execution of Nicky Kane" with Charles Webster, Cathy & Elliott Lewis, Alan Reed, Hans Conried, The Basil Adlam Orchestra. A plot to free a condemned man from the gallows involves a staged "execution" and a funeral parlor. ABC.

March 14, 1948 *Escape*
"Log of the Evening Star." A story of murder and madness, in the tradition of Inner Sanctum Mystery. Jack Webb and Alan Reed are among the supporting cast. CBS.

March 15, 1948 *The Lux Radio Theatre*
"Irish Eyes Are Smiling" with Dick Haymes, Jeanne Crain, Bill Johnstone and Alan Reed in the cast. An adaptation of the 1944 20th Century Fox film. Host is William Keighley. Sponsored by Lux. CBS.

April 3, 1948 *Suspense*
"Suspicion." Drama based on the short story of the same name by Dorothy L. Sayers. Cast includes Sam Jaffe, Lurene Tuttle and Alan Reed. CBS.

April 10, 1948 *Operation Nightmare: Chapter Two*
Thirty-minute radio special (a sequel to a special of the same name from 1947). George Jessel, Richard Widmark, Al Jolson and Alan Reed star in this docu-drama. ABC.

April 15, 1948 *The Family Theatre*
"Wanted: One Baby." A fantasy drama about a couple unable to conceive, and the husband's journey to the land where babies are born. Daws Butler and Alan Reed are among the supporting cast. Mutual Network.

April 26, 1948 *The Lux Radio Theatre*
"Dear Ruth" with William Holden, Joan Caulfield and Alan Reed in the cast. An adaptation of the classic 1947 Paramount Studios film of the same name. Host is William Keighley. Sponsored by Lux. CBS.

June 10, 1948 *Hallmark Playhouse*
"The Devil and Daniel Webster." This was the first show of the series. A New Hampshire lawyer has to go to trial in an effort to defeat the cons of The Devil himself. John McIntire and Alan Reed star. Sponsored by Hallmark. CBS.

June 13, 1948 *Shorty Bell*
Situation comedy starring Mickey Rooney as a newspaper reporter. Cast includes John Hoyt and Alan Reed. CBS.

June 15, 1948 *The Little Immigrant*
The date listed is the date of recording, not the date of broadcast. This is a 37-minute audition recording for what would become *Life With Luigi*. J. Carrol Naish and Alan Reed play the same roles they would play for a number of years on the comedy program. The same script was reused for the *Life With Luigi* series.

June 28, 1948 *Let George Do It*
Stars Bob Bailey as George Valentine, a freelance detective. Supporting cast includes Harry Bartell, Wally Maher and Alan Reed. Sponsored by Signal Oil and Chevron. Mutual Network.

July 18, 1948 *The Adventures Of Sam Spade*
"The Missing Newshawk Caper." Private detective Sam Spade (played by Howard Duff) is hired to find a reporter. When he tracks the man down, the reporter is found stabbed to death. Alan Reed is among the supporting cast. Sponsored by Wildroot Cream Oil. CBS.

August 11, 1948 *The Whistler*
"Enough Rope." A strangler uses a silk stocking as a weapon of choice. Cast includes Howard McNear and Alan Reed. CBS.

August 16, 1948 *Let George Do It*
Stars Bob Bailey as George Valentine, a freelance detective, investigating a haunted house. Supporting cast includes Howard McNear, Wally Maher and Alan Reed. Sponsored by Signal Oil and Chevron. Mutual Network.

August 27, 1948 - May 27, 1949 *The Life of Riley*
Situation comedy with William Bendix as Chester A. Riley. Alan Reed played a number of supporting roles on the series. Alan Reed, Jr. played Riley's son Junior for one season. Sponsored by Prell. NBC.

September 6, 1948 *The Lux Radio Theatre*
"Mr. Peabody and the Mermaid" with William Powell, Irene Hervey and Alan Reed in the cast. An adaptation of the Guy and Constance Jones novel. Host is William Keighley. Sponsored by Lux. CBS.

September 9, 1948 - July 7, 1949 *Sealtest Variety Theatre*
Weekly regular: Dorothy Lamour. Musical variety program. Guests included Bob Hope, Gregory Peck, Ronald Colman, Ed Gardner, Jim and Marian Jordan and Harold Peary. Alan Reed played supporting roles for various skits. Sponsored by Sealtest. NBC.

September 21, 1948 - January 4, 1949 *Life With Luigi*
J. Carroll Naish stars as Luigi Basco, an Italian immigrant who grew up on the outskirts of Rome and faces a clash of cultures as he tries to "make good" in America. Alan Reed played the weekly role of Pasquale, Luigi's sponsor in America, owner of Pasquale's Spaghetti Palace in the Little Italy section of Chicago. CBS.

October 1, 1948 - June 24, 1949 *The Eddie Cantor Pabst Blue Ribbon Show*
Weekly regular: Eddie Cantor. Musical comedy variety program. On occasion the series presented a comedy skit and Alan Reed was among the supporting cast. Broadcasts confirmed to have Reed among the cast: October 15, 1948, December 3, 1948 and December 10, 1948.

October 3, 1948 - June 26, 1949 *The Phil Harris - Alice Faye Show*
Weekly regulars: Phil Harris and Alice Faye. Situation comedy. Alan Reed was among the supporting cast on a number of episodes. Sponsored by Rexall. NBC. Broadcasts confirmed to have Reed among the cast: January 2, 1949, January 9, 1949, March 27, 1949 and April 24, 1949.

October 4, 1948 *June Is My Girl*
An audition recording for a series that never came to be. Diana Lynn stars as June, who works for an impoverished employment agency. Cast includes Harry Bartell, Parley Baer and Alan Reed. Intended for NBC. The date listed is the recording date, not the date of broadcast.

October 6, 1948 - June 29, 1949 *Duffy's Tavern*
Weekly regular: Ed Gardner. Situation comedy about the mishaps in a New York City tavern. Alan Reed plays the role of Clancy the cop on a recurring basis until February 1949 when he began playing the role on a weekly basis. Sponsored by Ipana. NBC.

October 7, 1948 *The Secret Life Of Walter Mitty*
Stars Eddie Albert and Margo. Supporting cast includes Frank Lovejoy and Alan Reed. NBC.

October 14, 1948 *The Family Theatre*
"Farewell to Birdie McKeesler." Executives at a law firm are faced with the brutal task of firing an employee who has not proven his worth. George Murphy is host. June Haver and Alan Reed are among the cast. Mutual Network.

November 2, 1948 - February 26, 1949 *The George O'Hanlon Show*
Comedy series. Lurene Tuttle and Alan Reed were among the cast. Exactly how many episodes Reed appeared in remains unknown. Mutual.

November 2, 1948 *Favorite Story*
"The Judgment of Paris." Drama based on the popular story of the same name. Cast includes Hans Conried and Alan Reed. Syndicated.

November 7, 1948 *The Prudential Family Hour Of Stars*
"The Deeper Shadow." A successful businessman has a hidden past. Cast includes Frank Lovejoy, Ray Milland and Alan Reed. Sponsored by Prudential Insurance. CBS.

November 8, 1948 *The Railroad Hour*
"Rio Rita." Based on the musical of the same name. Alan Reed played a supporting role for this production. Sponsored by the Association of American Railroads. ABC.

November 14, 1948 *The Charlie McCarthy Show*
Weekly regulars: Edgar Bergen and Charlie McCarthy. Alan Reed appears in a brief skit and Ken Carpenter's "Coffee Calypso" song. Sponsored by Chase and Sanborn. NBC.

November 17, 1948 *The Family Theatre*
"Mr. Carousel." After bragging about his position at Carnegie Hall to a beautiful woman, a man learns that he has lost his job. Jeanette MacDonald is the hostess. Jimmy Durante and Alan Reed are among the cast. Mutual Network.

November 27, 1948 - May 27, 1948 *The Adventures of Ellery Queen*
Quiz program with a weekly mystery skit. The program premiered on June 18, 1939, but it wasn't until this season that Alan Reed signed on to play a supporting role for every episode. ABC.

December 6, 1948 *The Railroad Hour*
"Girl Crazy." Based on the musical of the same name. Alan Reed played the role of Slick for this production. Sponsored by the Association of American Railroads. ABC.

1949 - 1951 Syndication *The Damon Runyon Theater*
Syndicated series that premiered over KFI in Los Angeles on January 11, 1949. The exact dates and times varied by stations across the country. A total of 52 episodes were created. Produced by Alan Ladd's Mayfair Productions, this drama series featured adaptations of Damon Runyon's classic short stories, and faithfully adapted fictional characters. Alan Reed played the recurring role of Little Mitzi for a number of episodes.

1949 - 1952 *The Adventures of Maisie*
Syndicated program produced by MGM Studios. A total of 78 episodes were produced and broadcast circa 1949-1952. Alan Reed was among the cast of supporting performers for a number of episodes.

Circa 1949 *Sam Pilgrim's Progress*
An audition recording made circa 1949. Similar to the Damon Runyon stories, this program dealt with the ups and downs of a New York City cab driver. Alan Reed is among the supporting cast. Originally intended for ABC, the series never came to be.

January 9, 1949 - September 25, 1949 *Life With Luigi*
J. Carroll Naish stars as Luigi Basco, an Italian immigrant who grew up on the outskirts of Rome and faced a clash of cultures as he tries to "make good" in America. Alan Reed played the weekly role of Pasquale, Luigi's sponsor in America, owner of Pasquale's Spaghetti Palace in the Little Italy section of Chicago. CBS.

January 17, 1949 *The Railroad Hour*
"Naughty Marietta." Based on the musical of the same name. Alan Reed played the role of Rudolfo for this production. Sponsored by the Association of American Railroads. ABC.

January 26, 1949 *The Family Theatre*
"Melancholy Clown." Biographical drama about the famous theatrical producer David Belasco. Lionel Barrymore, Dean Stockwell and Alan Reed are among the cast. Mutual network.

February 21, 1949 *The Railroad Hour*
"Lady, Be Good!" Based on the musical of the same name. Alan Reed played Attorney Rufus Park for this production. Sponsored by the Association of American Railroads. ABC.

February 27, 1949 *The Adventures Of Ozzie and Harriet*
Weekly regulars: Ozzie and Harriet Nelson. Supporting cast includes John Brown, Hans Conried, Alan Reed and Henry Blair.
Sponsored by International Silver. NBC.

February 28, 1949 *The Lux Radio Theatre*
"Apartment for Peggy" with Jeanne Crain, William Holden, Edmund Gwenn and Alan Reed in the cast. An adaptation of the 20th Century Fox movie of the same name. Host is William Keighley. Sponsored by Lux. CBS.

March 7, 1949 *The Lux Radio Theatre*
"Red River" with John Wayne, Joanne Dru, Walter Brennan, Jeff Chandler and Alan Reed in the cast. An adaptation of the movie of the same name. Host is William Keighley. Sponsored by Lux. CBS.

March 7, 1949 *The Railroad Hour*
"The Merry Widow." Based on the musical of the same name. Alan Reed plays Baron Popoff for this production. Sponsored by the Association of American Railroads. ABC.

March 14, 1949 *The Railroad Hour*
"Eileen." Based on the musical of the same name. Alan Reed plays a supporting role for this production. Sponsored by the Association of American Railroads. ABC.

April 1, 1949 *The Philip Morris Playhouse*
"Apology." A caring husband allows his wife to die under strange circumstances and then finds himself having to cope with the anger of his father-in-law. Supporting cast includes Cathy Lewis and Sidney Miller. Sponsored by Philip Morris. CBS.

April 2, 1949 *The Adventures Of Philip Marlowe*
"The Last Laugh." Gerald Mohr plays the title character in a mystery about the reading of a will, and the dead man getting the last laugh over his greedy relatives. Supporting cast includes Doris Singleton and Gerald Mohr. CBS.

April 20, 1949 *The Texaco Star Theatre*
Weekly regular: Milton Berle. Berle does a salute to baseball with skits and songs related to America's favorite sport. Charles Irving, John Gibson and Alan Reed are among the supporting actors. Sponsored by Texaco. ABC.

May 9, 1949 *The Lux Radio Theatre*
"The Paradine Case" with Joseph Cotton, Valli, Louis Jourdan and Alan Reed in the cast. An adaptation of the 1947 David O. Selznick production, which was directed by Alfred Hitchcock. Director of the radio version is Fred Mac-Kaye. Host is William Keighley. Sponsored by Lux. CBS.

May 16, 1949 *The Lux Radio Theatre*
"April Showers" with Jack Carson, Dorothy Lamour, Robert Alda, Bobby Ellis and Alan Reed in the cast. An adaptation of the movie of the same name. Host is William Keighley. Sponsored by Lux. CBS.

May 23, 1949 *The Lux Radio Theatre*
"To the Ends of the Earth" with Dick Powell, Signe Hasso and Alan Reed in the cast. An adaptation of the Columbia movie of the same name. Host is William Keighley. Sponsored by Lux. CBS.

May 30, 1949 *The Lux Radio Theatre*
"Anna and the King of Siam" with Irene Dunne, James Mason and Alan Reed in the cast. An adaptation of the 1946 20th Century Fox movie of the same name. Host is William Keighley. Sponsored by Lux. CBS.

June 20, 1949 *The Lux Radio Theatre*
"Merton of the Movies" with Mickey Rooney, Arlene Dahl and Alan Reed
in the cast. An adaptation of the stage play by George S. Kaufman and Marc
Connelly. Host is William Keighley. Sponsored by Lux. CBS.

August 13, 1949 *Smilin' Ed McConnell's Buster Brown Gang*
Ed McConnell tells the story of Robin Hood. Alan Reed is among the cast.
Reed played numerous roles during the years this program aired on Saturday
Morning. This is the only known episode that exists in recorded form that
features Reed, and the only confirmed broadcast date. Sponsored by Buster
Brown Shoes. NBC.

August 22, 1949 *Let George Do It*
"The Empress of Fish Falls." George Valentine finds the dead body of a midget
with three gunshots in the back. Stars Bob Bailey as Valentine. Supporting
cast includes Verna Felton, Howard McNear and Alan Reed. Sponsored by
Standard Oil (Chevron). Mutual-Don Lee Network.

August 29, 1949 - June 26, 1950 *My Friend Irma*
Situation comedy starring Marie Wilson as Irma Peterson, a stenographer by
trade, who often got into trouble. Her boss, Mr. Clyde, was played by Alan
Reed in most of the episodes. Sponsored by Pepsodent. CBS.

September 1, 1949 *Suspense*
"Nightmare." Guest stars Gregory Peck as a father seeking revenge on the hit-
and-run driver who was responsible for the death of his son. Supporting cast
included Howard McNear and Alan Reed. Sponsored by Auto-Lite. CBS.

September 10, 1949 *The Anacin Hollywood Star Theatre*
"Promise of Murder." Rita Lynn, Margaret O'Brien and Alan Reed in the
cast.Sponsored by Anacin and Bisodol Mints. NBC.

September 12, 1949 *The Lux Radio Theatre*
"Deep Waters" with Dana Andrews, Donna Reed, Anne Revere and Alan
Reed in the cast. An adaptation of the 1948 20th Century Fox movie of the
same name. Vera Miles appears as the intermission guest, a relatively new
star billed as a "starlet" in this broadcast. Host is William Keighley. Sponsored by Lux. CBS.

September 16, 1949 *This Is Your FBI*
"The Chinatown Shakedown." Mystery based on a true case from the files of
the FBI. Alan Reed and Stacy Harris in the cast. Sponsored by Equitable
Life Insurance. ABC.

September 18, 1949 - June 4, 1950 *The Phil Harris - Alice Faye Show*
Weekly regulars: Phil Harris and Alice Faye. Situation comedy. Alan Reed was among the supporting cast for a number of episodes. Sponsored by Rexall. NBC. Broadcasts confirmed to have Reed among the cast: November 27, 1949 and May 21, 1950.

September 26, 1949 *The Lux Radio Theatre*
"The Emperor Waltz" with Bing Crosby, Ann Blyth, Willard Waterman in the cast. An adaptation of the 1948 Paramount movie of the same name. Host is William Keighley. Sponsored by Lux. CBS.

September 27, 1949- June 13, 1950 *Life With Luigi*
J. Carroll Naish stars as Luigi Basco, an Italian immigrant who grew up on the outskirts of Rome and faces a clash of cultures as he tries to "make good" in America. Alan Reed played the weekly role of Pasquale, Luigi's sponsor in America, owner of Pasquale's Spaghetti Palace in the Little Italy section of Chicago. Sponsored by Wrigley. CBS.

October 7, 1949 - June 30, 1950 *The Life of Riley*
Situation comedy with William Bendix as Chester A. Riley. Alan Reed played a number of supporting roles on the series. Sponsored by Prell until March 10, 1950 when Pabst took over. NBC.

October 22, 1949 *Escape*
"Night in Havana." Based on the story by Burnham Carter about Cuban gun-running. Cast included Jack Webb, Jeff Corey and Alan Reed. CBS.

November 3, 1949 *Suspense*
"The Search for Isabelle." Guest star Red Skelton is plagued by a series of phone calls from various people asking for a woman he does not know. So he searches out the woman and unravels the mystery. Supporting cast includes William Conrad and Alan Reed. Sponsored by Auto-Lite. CBS.

November 7, 1949 *The Lux Radio Theatre*
"The High Wall" with Van Heflin, Janet Leigh, Gerald Mohr and Alan Reed in the cast. An adaptation of the 1947 MGM movie of the same name. Host is William Keighley. Sponsored by Lux. CBS.

November 19, 1949 *Broadway Is My Beat*
Cast includes Larry Thor, Joseph Kearns, Jerry Hausner and Alan Reed. CBS.

November 21, 1949 *The Lux Radio Theatre*
"Sorrowful Jones" with Bob Hope, Lucille Ball, Ed Begley and Alan Reed in the cast. An adaptation of the 1949 Paramount Pictures movie of the same name. Host is William Keighley. Sponsored by Lux. CBS.

November 21, 1949 *The Railroad Hour*
"No, No, Nanette." Based on the musical of the same name. Alan Reed played the role of James Smith for this production. Sponsored by the Association of American Railroads. NBC.

December 5, 1949 *The Lux Radio Theatre*
"Dear Ruth" with William Holden, Joan Caulfield, Mona Freeman and Alan Reed in the cast. An adaptation of the 1947 Paramount Pictures movie of the same name. Host is William Keighley. Sponsored by Lux. CBS.

December 19, 1949 *The Lux Radio Theatre*
"The Bishop's Wife" with Tyrone Power, David Niven, Jane Greer and Alan Reed in the cast. An adaptation of the 1947 Samuel Golwyn/RKO movie of the same name. Host is William Keighley. Sponsored by Lux. CBS.

December 26, 1949 *The Lux Radio Theatre*
"My Dream is Yours" with Jack Carson, June Haver, Betty Lou Gerson and Alan Reed in the cast. An adaptation of the 1949 Warner Bros. movie of the same name. Host is William Keighley. Sponsored by Lux. CBS.

January 22, 1950 - April 30, 1950 *The Adventures of Christopher London*
Adventure series about Christopher London, a globetrotting investigator-troubleshooter who tackled a weekly "excursion against crime." Glenn Ford plays the lead. Supporting players on an almost-weekly basis included Virginia Gregg, Ted de Corsia and Alan Reed. NBC.

February 6, 1950 *The Lux Radio Theatre*
"Red, Hot and Blue" with Betty Hutton, John Lund, William Conrad and Alan Reed in the cast. An adaptation of the 1949 Paramount Pictures movie of the same name. Host is William Keighley. Sponsored by Lux. CBS.

February 17, 1950 *Screen Director's Playhouse*
"It's in the Bag." A dramatization of the motion picture of the same name. Among the cast: Fred Allen, John Brown, Lurene Tuttle, Hans Conried, Sheldon Leonard and Alan Reed. Sponsored by RCA. NBC.

February 23, 1950 *Suspense*
"Slow Burn." A professional prize fighter decides to exact revenge against the man who stole his girl. Stars Dick Powell; Wally Maher and Alan Reed are in the supporting cast. Sponsored by Auto-Lite. CBS.

March 2, 1950 *The Hallmark Playhouse*
"The Indestructible Julia." A single, older woman rejects all options for a love life so she can devote her free time to her sister's children. Katina Paxinou and Alan Reed are among the cast. Sponsored by Hallmark. CBS.

March 6, 1950 *The Lux Radio Theatre*
"Slatterly's Romance" with Richard Conte, Maureen O'Hara, Veronica Lake and Alan Reed in the cast. An adaptation of the 1949 20th Century Fox movie of the same name. Host is William Keighley. Sponsored by Lux. CBS.

March 27, 1950 *Let George Do It*
"The Tears of Sorrow." George Valentine investigates the origin of a corpse in a silver coffin. Supporting cast includes Virginia Gregg, Larry Dobkin and Alan Reed. Sponsored by Standard Oil (Chevron). Mutual-Don Lee Network.

March 31, 1950 *The Halls Of Ivy*
Weekly regulars: Ronald Colman and Benita Hume. Supporting cast includes Gloria Gordon and Alan Reed. Sponsored by Schlitz Beer. NBC.

April 23, 1950 *The Amos 'n' Andy Show*
Weekly regulars: Freeman Gosden and Charles Correll. The Kingfish loses all his money and the tickets to a lodge meet in Chicago, forcing him and Andy to hitch-hike home. Sponsored by Rinso. CBS.

April 27, 1950 *Suspense*
"The Chain." Guest stars Agnes Moorehead as a spinster who sends a series of chain letters that cause a riot. Supporting cast includes William Conrad and Alan Reed. Sponsored by Auto-Lite. CBS.

May 8, 1950 *The Lux Radio Theatre*
"The Life of Riley" with William Bendix, John Brown and Alan Reed in the cast. Based on the 1949 movie, which was based on the radio series of the same name. Host is William Keighley. Sponsored by Lux. CBS.

May 8, 1950 - June 5, 1950 *The Adventures of Christopher London*
Adventure series about Christopher London, a globetrotting investigator-troubleshooter who tackled a weekly "excursion against crime." Glenn Ford plays the lead. Supporting players on an almost-weekly basis included Virginia Gregg, Ted de Corsia and Alan Reed. NBC.

May 15, 1950 *The Lux Radio Theatre*
"The Lady Takes a Sailor" with Jane Wyman, Dennis Morgan and Alan Reed in the cast. An adaptation of the 1949 Warner Bros. movie of the same name. Host is William Keighley. Sponsored by Lux. CBS.

May 25, 1950 *Suspense*
"Very Much Like a Nightmare." Guest stars Dennis O'Keefe as a man who awakens in his office building to find himself witness to a theft. Supporting cast includes Howard McNear and Alan Reed. Sponsored by Auto-Lite. CBS.

June 26, 1950 *Let George Do It*
"Most Likely to Die." A practical joke at a college backfires. George Valentine investigates. Supporting cast includes Wally Maher, Larry Dobkin and Alan Reed. Sponsored by Standard Oil (Chevron). Mutual-Don Lee Network.

July 5, 1950 *The Halls Of Ivy*
Weekly regulars: Ronald Colman and Benita Hume. Alan Reed plays a character named "The Moose." Sponsored by Schlitz Beer. NBC.

July 17, 1950 *The Gentleman*
"The Episode of the Lovely Liar." This was an audition recording for a proposed NBC series that never came to be. The date listed is the recording date, not the broadcast date. Stars Reginald Gardiner. Alan Reed is among the supporting cast.

August 15, 1950 - July 3, 1951 *Life With Luigi*
J. Carroll Naish stars as Luigi Basco, an Italian immigrant who grew up on the outskirts of Rome and faces a clash of cultures as he tries to "make good" in America. Alan Reed played the weekly role of Pasquale, Luigi's sponsor in America, owner of Pasquale's Spaghetti Palace in the Little Italy section of Chicago. Sponsored by Wrigley. CBS.

September 14, 1950 - June 25, 1951 *My Friend Irma.*
Situation comedy starring Marie Wilson as Irma Peterson, a stenographer by trade, who often got into trouble. Her boss, Mr. Clyde, was played by Alan Reed in most of the episodes. Sponsored by Pepsodent. CBS.

September 18, 1950 - December 28, 1950 *Falstaff's Fables*
Children's program with Alan Reed Sr. and Jr. 5-minute program, broadcast
five-times-a-week. Sponsored by Mars. ABC.

October 1, 1950 - January 28, 1951 *The Phil Harris - Alice Faye Show*
Weekly regulars: Phil Harris and Alice Faye. Situation comedy. Alan Reed was
among the supporting cast for a number of episodes. NBC.

October 1, 1950 *The Amos 'n' Andy Show*
Weekly regulars: Freeman Gosden and Charles Correll. Kingfish has been drafted
and attempts to get out of the mix-up. Alan Reed is among the supporting
cast. Sponsored by Rinso. CBS.

October 6, 1950 - June 29, 1951 *The Life of Riley*
Situation comedy with William Bendix as Chester A. Riley. Alan Reed played
a number of supporting roles on the series. Sponsored by Pabst. NBC.

October 27, 1950 *The Man Called X*
"Journey to Xenophon." Herbert Marshall is a secret agent out to find a cure
for cancer. Supporting cast includes Alan Reed and Dan O'Herlihy. NBC.

November 10, 1950 - November 10, 1951 *The Magnificent Montague*
Situation comedy starring Monte Wooley as a washed-up Shakespearean
actor. Alan Reed played a supporting role on occasion. Confirmed dates
of broadcast with Reed in the cast: January 19, 1951, January 26, 1951 and
February 2, 1951.

November 20, 1950 *Let George Do It*
"Cause for Thanksgiving." A ten-year old is unable to speak and George suspect
s foul play. Supporting cast includes Wally Maher, Virginia Gregg and Alan
Reed. Sponsored by Standard Oil (Chevron). Mutual-Don Lee Network.

December 3, 1950 *Hedda Hopper's Hollywood*
Weekly regular: Hedda Hopper (also known as *The Hedda Hopper Show*). Musical,
variety, interviews and gossip. Guests Richard Widmark and Victor Mature
recreate a scene from the movie Kiss of Death. Alan Reed is among the supporting cast. NBC.

January 8, 1951 *The Lux Radio Theatre*
"Once More, My Darling" with Ann Blyth, Van Heflin, Janet Scott and Alan
Reed in the cast. An adaptation of the 1949 Universal-International movie
of the same name. Host is William Keighley. Sponsored by Lux. CBS.

January 17, 1951 *The Family Theatre*
"The Golden Touch." Guests Jack Benny, Norma Felton, Mel Blanc and Frank Nelson present a retelling of the King Midas story. Alan Reed is among the cast. Mutual Network.

January 20, 1951 *My Favorite Husband*
Situation comedy starring Lucille Ball and Richard Denning as Liz and George Cooper. Based on the novel Mr. and Mrs. Cugat by Isabel Scott Rorick. Alan Reed is among the supporting cast.

January 21, 1951 *Hedda Hopper's Hollywood*
Weekly regular: Hedda Hopper (also known as *The Hedda Hopper Show*). Musical, variety, interviews and gossip. Guest Loretta Young performs a scene from her latest movie. Alan Reed is among the supporting cast. NBC.

January 21, 1951 - June 17, 1951 *Mr. and Mrs. Blandings*
Weekly regulars: Cary Grant and Betsy Drake. Situation comedy based on the motion picture of the same name. Alan Reed played a supporting role for a number of episodes. Sponsored by TWA. NBC.

January 31, 1951 *The Family Theatre*
"The Adventures of Pinocchio." Joan Leslie is guest hostess and narrator. Mel Blanc offers his rendition of the classic children's story. Howard McNear and Alan Reed are among the cast. Mutual Network.

February 3, 1951 *My Favorite Husband*
Situation comedy starring Lucille Ball and Richard Denning as Liz and George Cooper. Based on the novel Mr. and Mrs. Cugat by Isabel Scott Rorick. Alan Reed is among the supporting cast.

February 4, 1951 - May 27, 1951 *The Phil Harris - Alice Faye Show*
Weekly regulars: Phil Harris and Alice Faye. Situation comedy. Alan Reed was among the supporting cast for a number of episodes. Sponsored by RCA. NBC.

March 26, 1951 *The Lux Radio Theatre*
"Seventh Heaven" with Janet Gaynor, Charles Farrell and Alan Reed in the cast. An adaptation of the 1922 stage play by Austin Strong. The leads (Gaynor and Farrell) starred in the popular 1927 silent film version. Host is William Keighley. Sponsored by Lux. CBS.

April 11, 1951 *The Family Theatre*
"General Pumpkin's Holiday." Guest Arthur Lake channels his Dagwood screen character for this slapstick comedy about a man who creates his own holiday. Charlie Ruggles is the guest host. Alan Reed is among the cast. Mutual Network.

May 23, 1951 *The Family Theatre*
"The Golden Touch." Lucille Ball is the guest hostess. The entire cast from the January 31, 1951 broadcast perform the same script from five months earlier. Mutual Network.

June 8, 1951 *Nightbeat*
Frank Lovejoy stars as Randy Stone, a newspaper journalist who is roaming the streets for a man who has been bitten by a rabid dog, and is unaware of it. Supposedly Alan Reed is in the supporting cast, but this has not been verified. NBC.

June 25, 1951 *The Lux Radio Theatre*
"The Reformer and the Redhead" with June Allyson, Dick Powell and Alan Reed in the cast. An adaptation of the 1952 MGM movie of the same name. Host is William Keighley. Sponsored by Lux. CBS.

August 28, 1951 - May 27, 1952 *Life With Luigi*
J. Carroll Naish stars as Luigi Basco, an Italian immigrant who grew up on the outskirts of Rome and faces a clash of cultures as he tries to "make good" in America. Alan Reed played the weekly role of Pasquale, Luigi's sponsor in America, owner of Pasquale's Spaghetti Palace in the Little Italy section of Chicago. Sponsored by Wrigley. CBS.

September 20, 1951 *Hollywood Star Playhouse*
"Hour of Truth." In the bull fight ring, an older man decides to do one last fight to the death. Supporting cast includes Gerald Mohr, Harry Bartell and Alan Reed. ABC.

September 30, 1951 *Wild Bill Hickok*
"The Fury of Savage River." Stars Guy Madison and Andy Devine. Supporting cast includes Wally Maher and Alan Reed. Sponsored by Kellogg's. Mutual Network.

September 30, 1951 - May 25, 1952 *The Phil Harris - Alice Faye Show*
Weekly regulars: Phil Harris and Alice Faye. Situation comedy. Alan Reed was among the supporting cast for a number of episodes. Sponsored by RCA. NBC.

October 5, 1951 - June 27, 1952 *Richard Diamond, Private Detective*
Detective series starring Dick Powell. Alan Reed played a number of supporting roles throughout the series. The show premiered April 24, 1949 but it wasn't until this particular season that Reed became an almost regular for the series.

October 14, 1951 - June 15, 1952 *My Friend Irma*
Situation comedy starring Marie Wilson as Irma Peterson, a stenographer by trade, who often got into trouble. Her boss, Mr. Clyde, was played by Alan Reed in most of the episodes. Sponsored by Pearson. CBS.

January 10, 1952 - July 3, 1952 *The Modern Adventures of Casanova*
Romance thriller "based upon an idea by and starring Errol Flynn." Flynn played Christopher Casanova, lover and secret agent. He was an agent for the "World Criminal Police Commission." Alan Reed was a supporting performer for a number of episodes. Syndicated across the country heard at various times on various radio stations. The dates listed correspond to the Mutual Network.

May 12, 1952 *The Lux Radio Theatre*
"Riding High" with Fred MacMurray, Rhonda Fleming, Scatman Crothers and Alan Reed in the cast. An adaptation of the 1950 Paramount Pictures movie of the same name. Host is William Keighley. Sponsored by Lux. CBS.

June 8, 1952 - September 7, 1952 *December Bride*
Alan Reed played a number of supporting roles in this situation comedy about Lily Ruskin (Spring Byington), a widow in search of a husband. Based on the character created by Parke Levy. CBS.

August 12, 1952 - May 3, 1953 *Life With Luigi*
J. Carroll Naish stars as Luigi Basco, an Italian immigrant who grew up on the outskirts of Rome and faces a clash of cultures as he tries to "make good" in America. Alan Reed played the weekly role of Pasquale, Luigi's sponsor in America, owner of Pasquale's Spaghetti Palace in the Little Italy section of Chicago. Sponsored by Wrigley. CBS.

September 26, 1952 *The Cascade Of Stars*
NBC radio special celebrating the new season of programs. Cast includes Red Skelton, Groucho Marx, Phil Harris and Alan Reed. NBC.

October 2, 1952 - December 25, 1952 *The Modern Adventures of Casanova*
Romance thriller "based upon an idea by and starring Errol Flynn." Flynn played Christopher Casanova, lover and secret agent. He was an agent for the "World Criminal Police Commission." Alan Reed was a supporting performer for a number of episodes. Syndicated across the country heard at various times on various radio stations. The dates listed correspond to the Mutual Network.

October 5, 1952 - June 28, 1953 *The Phil Harris - Alice Faye Show*
Weekly regulars: Phil Harris and Alice Faye. Situation comedy. Alan Reed was among the supporting cast for a number of episodes. Sponsored by RCA. NBC.

October 7, 1952 - June 30, 1953 *My Friend Irma*
Situation comedy starring Marie Wilson as Irma Peterson, a stenographer by trade, who often got into trouble. Her boss, Mr. Clyde, was played by Alan Reed in most of the episodes. Sponsored by Camel Cigarettes. CBS.

October 12, 1952 - February 15, 1953 *December Bride*
Alan Reed played a number of supporting roles in this situation comedy about Lily Ruskin (Spring Byington), a widow in search of a husband. Based on the character created by Parke Levy. CBS.

February 25, 1953 - May 27, 1953 *December Bride*
Alan Reed played a number of supporting roles in this situation comedy about Lily Ruskin (Spring Byington), a widow in search of a husband. Based on the character created by Parke Levy. CBS.

April 2, 1953 *On Stage*
Anthology series of varied dramas. Alan Reed, Sammy Hill and Junius Matthews play roles in an adaptation of the classic, "The Lady or the Tiger."

April 4, 1953 *Broadway Is My Beat*
The waters of New York City wash up two dead bodies so the police investigate. Cast includes: Larry Thor, Charles Calvert, Jack Kruschen and Alan Reed. CBS.

May 10, 1953 *Escape*
"The Vessel of Wrath." Based on the Somerset Maugham story. Supporting cast includes Jeanette Nolan, Eric Snowden and Alan Reed. CBS.

June 7, 1953 - September 6, 1953 *December Bride*
Alan Reed played a number of supporting roles in this situation comedy about
Lily Ruskin (Spring Byington), a widow in search of a husband. Based on
the character created by Parke Levy. CBS.

July 11, 1953 *Stars Over Hollywood*
"I Give You Maggie." Ronald Reagan stars as a struggling writer. Supporting cast includes John Stevenson, Lurene Tuttle and Alan Reed. Sponsored
by Carnation Milk. CBS.

September 18, 1953 - June 18, 1954 *The Phil Harris - Alice Faye Show*
Weekly regulars: Phil Harris and Alice Faye. Situation comedy. Alan Reed was
among the supporting cast for a number of episodes. Sponsored by RCA.
NBC. Broadcasts confirmed to have Reed in the cast: October 16, 1953.

October 11, 1953 *The Hallmark Hall of Fame*
"Edwin L. Drake." Biography about the first man to ever drill for oil. Host
is Lionel Barrymore. Supporting cast includes John Dehner and Alan Reed.
Sponsored by Hallmark. CBS.

October 25, 1953 *The Hallmark Hall of Fame*
"Robert Livingstone." Drama about the negotiations involved for the famed
Louisiana Purchase. Host is Lionel Barrymore. Supporting cast includes
William Conrad and Alan Reed. Sponsored by Hallmark. CBS.

October 30, 1953 *Wild Bill Hickok*
"Shotgun Gang." Hickok and Jingles run into an ambush when they attempt
to track down a gang of thieves. Stars Guy Madison and Andy Devine. Supporting cast includes Byron Kane and Alan Reed. Sponsored by Kellogg's.
Mutual Network.

November 29, 1953 *The Six Shooter*
Western series starring James Stewart as Britt Ponset, a loner wandering
the plains. Alan Reed was among the supporting cast in the titled "Sheriff
Billy."

December 1, 1953 - August 23, 1954 *My Friend Irma*
Situation comedy starring Marie Wilson as Irma Peterson, a stenographer by
trade, who often got into trouble. Her boss, Mr. Clyde, was played by Alan
Reed in most of the episodes. Multiple sponsors. CBS.

December 18, 1953 *Wild Bill Hickok*
"Seven Silver Bullets." A man living alone in a cabin is shot by a single silver bullet. Stars Guy Madison and Andy Devine. Supporting cast includes Vic Perrin and Alan Reed. Sponsored by Kellogg's. Mutual Network.

December 24, 1953 *Meet Mr. McNutley*
Comedy series with Ray Milland as professor Ray McNulty, an English professor at a girl's college. Alan Reed in a supporting role. Sponsored by General Electric. CBS.

Circa 1954 *The U. N. Story*
"Chico and the F.A.O." True story of how the United Nations helped Mexican breeders develop a mountain-hardy breed of cattle. Cast includes Arnold Stang and Alan Reed. Syndicated.

1954 Syndication *Life With Luigi*
J. Carroll Naish stars as Luigi Basco, an Italian immigrant who grew up on the outskirts of Rome and faces a clash of cultures as he tries to "make good" in America. Alan Reed played the weekly role of Pasquale, Luigi's sponsor in America, owner of Pasquale's Spaghetti Palace in the Little Italy section of Chicago. 15-minute series for syndication. CBS.

January 8, 1954 - May 21, 1954 *That's Rich*
Stan Freberg plays the role of Richard E. Wilk, who worked for B.B. Hackett's Consolidated Paper Products Company. This situation comedy featured a cast of weekly regulars in supporting roles including Frank Nelson, Daws Butler, Hal March and Alan Reed. CBS.

March 26, 1954 *Wild Bill Hickok*
"The Fury of the Wind." A gunman is paid $4,000 to hunt and kill Wild Bill. Stars Guy Madison and Andy Devine. Supporting cast includes Vic Perrin and Alan Reed. Sponsored by Kellogg's. Mutual Network.

July 15, 1954 - September 23, 1954 *That's Rich*
Stan Freberg plays the role of Richard E. Wilk, who worked for B.B. Hackett's Consolidated Paper Products Company. This situation comedy featured a cast of weekly regulars in supporting roles including Frank Nelson, Daws Butler, Hal March and Alan Reed. CBS.

October 12, 1954 *The Lux Radio Theatre*
"Great Expectations" with Rock Hudson, Barbara Rush, William Conrad and Alan Reed in the cast. An adaptation of the 1946 movie of the same name. Host is Irving Cummings. Sponsored by Lux. CBS.

October 15, 1954 *Wild Bill Hickok*
"Satan at the Circus." A series of accidents at the circus give Wild Bill cause to investigate. Stars Guy Madison and Andy Devine. Supporting cast includes Jeff Silver, Dick Beals and GeGe Pearson and Alan Reed. Sponsored by Kellogg's. Mutual Network.

October 26, 1954 *The Lux Radio Theatre*
"The Song of Bernadette" with Ann Blyth, Charles Bickford, William Conrad and Alan Reed in the cast. An adaptation of the 1943 movie of the same name. Host is Irving Cummings. Sponsored by Lux. CBS.

November 9, 1954 *The Lux Radio Theatre*
"My Man Godfrey" with Jeff Chandler, Julie Adams and Alan Reed in the cast. An adaptation of the 1936 Universal Studios movie of the same name. Host is Irving Cummings. Sponsored by Lux. CBS.

March 16, 1955 *The Family Theatre*
"Double Crossing." Three smugglers on board a luxury liner face off against a little girl who eats dog biscuits. Esther Williams is the guest hostess. Richard Denning, Charlotte Lawrence and Alan Reed are among the cast. Mutual Network.

May 29, 1956 *Biography In Sound*
"A Portrait of Fred Allen." A documentary/biography of humorist Fred Allen. Guests include Jack Benny, Tallulah Bankhead, James Mason, Jimmy Durante, Edgar Bergen, Goodman Ace and Alan Reed. NBC.

June 4, 1956 - June 8, 1956 *Yours Truly, Johnny Dollar*
"The Indestructible Mike Matter." Five-part story about an insurance investigator trying to solve a mystery involving a man who apparently has nine lives. Among the supporting cast: Larry Dobkin, Howard McNear and Alan Reed. CBS.

August 3, 1956 *The CBS Radio Workshop*
"Subways Are For Sleeping." Fictional story about a homeless man. Frank Gerstle, Sarah Selby and Alan Reed are among the cast. CBS.

August 31, 1956 *The CBS Radio Workshop*
"Colloquy Three: An Analysis of Satire." Stan Freberg demonstrates the art of satire by playing excerpts from his recordings. Daws Butler, Parley Baer, June Foray and Alan Reed are among the cast. CBS.

September 14, 1956 *The CBS Radio Workshop*
"A Pride of Carrots or Venus Well Served." A crew of astronauts from the planet Earth land on Venus with vegetables. June Foray, Daws Butler and Alan Reed are among the cast. CBS.

December 5, 1956 *Recollections At Thirty*
A recording from a Baby Snooks skit from the 1930s is played for the radio audience, to feature Alan Reed as "Daddy." NBC.

July 28, 1957 *Suspense*
"Murder on Mike." An author of radio scripts for a murder/mystery program decides to exact revenge against his vile director. Supporting cast includes Raymond Burr and Alan Reed. Sponsored by Kent Cigarettes. CBS.

September 15, 1957 *Yours Truly, Johnny Dollar*
"The JPD Matter." Bob Bailey plays Johnny Dollar, an insurance investigator. Beer companies rival for the dominating spot and a scheme involving dynamite is plotted. Supporting cast includes Jeanne Bates and Alan Reed. CBS.

December 1, 1957 *Heartbeat Theatre*
"Yuletide Embers." Supporting cast includes Parley Baer and Alan Reed. Sponsored by the Salvation Army. Syndicated.

February 23, 1958 *Yours Truly, Johnny Dollar*
"The Durango Laramie Matter." An eccentric who washes hundred dollar bills goes missing and Dollar seeks out the culprit. Supporting cast includes Virginia Gregg, Alan Reed and John McIntire. CBS.

April 13, 1958 *Yours Truly, Johnny Dollar*
"The Wayward Money Matter." A tobacco company has been robbed and Dollar investigates the books — and the suspects. Supporting cast includes Vic Perrin, Virginia Gregg and Alan Reed. CBS.

April 20, 1958 *Yours Truly, Johnny Dollar*
"The Wayward Trout Matter." Supporting cast includes Larry Dobkin, Edgar Barrier, Russell Thorsen and Alan Reed. CBS.

July 13, 1958 *Yours Truly, Johnny Dollar*
"The Mojave Red Matter" (Part One). A boat sinks and a man named Red is the prime suspect. Murder also occurs and Johnny Dollar, an insurance investigator, digs into the facts of the case. Supporting cast includes Forrest Lewis, Parley Baer, Barney Phillips and Alan Reed. CBS.

July 20, 1958 *Yours Truly, Johnny Dollar*
"The Mojave Red Matter" (Part Two). A boat sinks and a man named Red is the prime suspect. Murder also occurs and Johnny Dollar, an insurance investigator, digs into the facts of the case. Supporting cast includes Forrest Lewis, Parley Baer, Barney Phillips and Alan Reed. CBS.

August 10, 1958 *Heartbeat Theatre*
"A Matter of Life." Alan Reed plays the role of an Irish cop. Sponsored by the Salvation Army. CBS.

January 11, 1959 *Yours Truly, Johnny Dollar*
"The Deadly Doubt Matter." Bob Bailey plays Johnny Dollar, an insurance investigator who seeks an alibi for a woman in distress. Supporting cast includes Paul Dubov, Virginia Gregg and Alan Reed. CBS.

January 25, 1959 *Suspense*
"Four of a Kind." A hitch-hiker plays a silly game called "License Plate Poker." Supporting cast includes Barney Phillips, Elliott Reid and Alan Reed. CBS.

April 5, 1959 *Yours Truly, Johnny Dollar*
"The Frisco Fire Matter." Johnny seeks the man responsible for the death of a friend, who also happens to be an arsonist. Supporting cast includes Larry Dobkin, Vic Perrin and Alan Reed. Sponsored by Look Magazine, Fram Filters and Lysol. CBS.

May 17, 1959 *Yours Truly, Johnny Dollar*
"The Twin Trouble Matter." The twin brother of one of Johnny's clients is being blackmailed. Supporting cast includes Frank Gerstle and Alan Reed. CBS.

July 5, 1959 *Yours Truly, Johnny Dollar*
"The Only One Butt Matter." A clue in an ashtray helps Johnny discover the whereabouts of a missing woman. Supporting cast includes Virginia Gregg, Alan Reed and Herb Vigran. CBS.

December 13, 1959 *Heartbeat Theatre*
"Humbug." Alan Reed plays a rich old man who despises the Christmas holiday. Sponsored by the Salvation Army. Syndicated.

December 20, 1959 *Yours Truly, Johnny Dollar*
"The Red Mystery Matter." Johnny's favorite fishing guide turns up missing. Sponsored by Fitch Shampoo and Winston Cigarettes. CBS.

April 2, 1961 *Heartbeat Theatre*
"The Coin." Alan Reed plays the role of a writer who comes across a coin involved in the life of Christ. Sponsored by the Salvation Army. Syndicated.

February 18, 1962 *Heartbeat Theatre*
"The Prisoner." Alan Reed plays a man who likes to think of himself as a notorious criminal, until a Salvation Army officer convinces him otherwise. Sponsored by the Salvation Army. Syndicated.

March 18, 1962 *Heartbeat Theatre*
"Gang War." Alan Reed appears in the cast as a Salvation Army officer who sets out to smash a street gang of delinquents. Sponsored by the Salvation Army. Syndicated.

June 3, 1962 *Heartbeat Theatre*
"The Gateway." A prisoner in an Argentine jail is given a second chance on life Alan Reed is in the cast. Sponsored by the Salvation Army. Syndicated.

December 23, 1962 *Heartbeat Theatre*
"Christmas Leave." A World War II soldier goes A.W.O.L. in order to show his wife Christmas in New York City. Sponsored by the Salvation Army. Syndicated.

April 21, 1963 *Heartbeat Theatre*
"The Man Who Found Himself." An alcoholic discovers he has a secret past. Sponsored by the Salvation Army. Syndicated.

September 22, 1963 *Heartbeat Theatre*
"No Place to Go." A baseball player hooks on to a get-rich-quick scheme. Sponsored by the Salvation Army. Syndicated.

January 5, 1964 *Heartbeat Theatre*
Cast includes Jay Jostyn and Alan Reed. Sponsored by the Salvation Army. Syndicated.

June 7, 1964 *Heartbeat Theatre*
"Chicken on a Treadmill." Teens like to play chicken in the road with their hot rods, and some prove to be fatal. Sponsored by the Salvation Army. Syndicated.

July 12, 1964 *Heartbeat Theatre*
"Neither Sorrow Nor Crying." Sponsored by the Salvation Army. Syndicated.

September 20, 1964 *Heartbeat Theatre*
"Vacation With Pay." After seven years hard work, a Salvation Army couple believe they are going on their first true vacation…or so they think. Sponsored by the Salvation Army. Syndicated.

October 17, 1964 *Arch Oboler's Plays*
"Special to Hollywood." When the engines of an airplane stop, the passengers discover they remain suspended in mid-air. Cast includes Gloria Blondell and Alan Reed. Syndicated.

January 24, 1965 *Heartbeat Theatre*
"The Calling of Soong Yung." A young Chinese-American discovers that prejudice gets him nowhere. His way of thinking is changed courtesy of the Salvation Army. Sponsored by the Salvation Army. Syndicated.

August 8, 1965 *Heartbeat Theatre*
"The Name of the Game." Sponsored by the Salvation Army. Syndicated.

October 16, 1966 *Heartbeat Theatre*
"A Whole New World." A father resents his teenage son when he discovers the boy makes more in three hours of work after school hours than he made in a week during the depression. Cast includes Marvin Miller, Jane Webb and Alan Reed. Sponsored by the Salvation Army. Syndicated.

October 23, 1966 *Heartbeat Theatre*
"Only You Can Do It Yourself." When a man walks out of a 20-year marriage, the Salvation Army becomes involved. Cast includes Peggy Webber and Alan Reed. Sponsored by the Salvation Army. Syndicated.

December 18, 1966 *Heartbeat Theatre*
"Christmas Wedding." A young couple wants to get married on Christmas Eve. Sponsored by the Salvation Army. Syndicated.

January 2, 1972 *Same Time, Same Station*
Features a rebroadcast of the Favorite Story episode titled "The Judgment of Paris" with Alan Reed in the cast.

January 9, 1972 *Same Time, Same Station*
This episode features Alan Reed recollecting his fond days on old-time radio, with featured clips from various recordings of the past.

April 2, 1972 *Same Time, Same Station*
Features a number of radio bloopers with a cast of dozens including Alan Reed.

May 21, 1972 *Same Time, Same Station*
Features a rebroadcast of many Eddie Cantor radio programs. Alan Reed is among the cast.

May 28, 1972 *Same Time, Same Station*
Features a rebroadcast of many Eddie Cantor radio programs. Alan Reed is among the cast.

September 30, 1973 *Same Time, Same Station*
A tribute to Fred Allen with recordings from the past. Alan Reed is among the cast.

October 8, 1973 - October 12, 1973 *The Hollywood Radio Theatre*
"But I Wouldn't Want to Die There." Five-part story about a reporter trying to unearth the facts behind a murder case. Rod Serling is the host. Nehemiah Persoff and Alan Reed are among the cast. Various sponsors. Mutual Network.

October 7, 1974 *The CBS Radio Mystery Theater*
"Sister of Death." Anita Sutcliffe buys a painting at an auction and soon discovers that it is a portrait of her husband's former wife, who had been murdered during a robbery. With K.T. Stevens and Alan Reed in the cast. CBS.

September 15, 1975 *The CBS Radio Mystery Theater*
"The Little Old Lady Killer." A woman detective attempts to beat the police to the solution of a mystery involving a killer on the prowl. With Diane Baker and Alan Reed in the cast. CBS.

FILM SHORT SUBJECTS

1934 Rambling 'Round Radio Row No. 3 *(Vitaphone/Warner Bros.)*
1936 Teddy Bergman's International Broadcast *(Mentone/Universal)*
1937 Porky's Romance *(Warner Bros.)*
1937 Teddy Bergman's Bar-B-Q *(Mentone/Universal)*
1952 Teachers Are People *(Disney)*
1952 Two Weeks' Vacation *(Disney)*
1953 Father's Day Off *(Disney)*

FILM

1944 Days of Glory *(RKO)*
1945 Nob Hill *(20th Century-Fox)*
1946 The Postman Always Rings Twice *(MGM)*
1950 Perfect Strangers *(Warner Bros.)*
1950 Emergency Wedding *(Columbia)*
1951 The Redhead and the Cowboy *(Paramount)*
1951 Here Comes the Groom *(Paramount)*
1952 Viva Zapata! *(20th Century-Fox)*
1952 Actors and Sin *(United Artists)*
1953 I, the Jury *(United Artists)*
1954 Geraldine *(Republic)*
1954 Woman's World *(20th Century-Fox)*
1955 The Far Horizons/Untamed West *(Paramount)*
1955 Lady and the Tramp *(Disney)*
1955 Kiss of Fire *(Universal-International)*
1955 Desperate Hours *(Paramount)*
1956 Time Table *(United Artists)*
1956 The Revolt of Mamie Stover *(20th Century-Fox)*
1956 He Laughed Last *(Columbia)*
1958 The Tarnished Angels *(Universal-International)*
1958 Marjorie Morningstar *(Warner Bros.)*
1959 1001 Arabian Nights/Magoo's Arabian Nights *(UPA/Columbia)*
1961 Breakfast at Tiffany's *(Paramount)*
1966 The Man Called Flintstone *(Hanna-Barbera/Columbia)*
1969 A Dream of Kings *(National General)*
1971 Shinbone Alley *(Fine Arts/Allied Artists)*
1978 The Seniors *(Cinema Shares)*

TELEVISION

Your Show Time ("The Treasure of Franchard") March 18, 1949
The Buster Brown TV Show with Smilin' Ed McConnell and the Buster Brown Gang August 26, 1950 – April 23, 1955
Life with Luigi September 22, 1952 – December 29, 1952
Duffy's Tavern May 4, 1954 – October 26, 1954
The Public Defender ("The Clown") 1954
The Ray Bolger Show October 8, 1954
Make Room for Daddy ("Danny Lands in Pictures") November 2, 1954
Make Room for Daddy ("Big Nose") November 9, 1954
Make Room for Daddy ("The Anna Maria Alberghetti Show")
    December 21, 1954
TV Reader's Digest ("How Charlie Faust Won a Pennant for the Giants")
    April 11, 1955
Goodyear TV Playhouse ("Visit to a Small Planet") May 8, 1955
Damon Runyon Theater ("Old Em's Kentucky Home") May 28, 1955
Big Town ("Comic Book Murder") June 8, 1955
Andy's Gang August 20, 1955 – December 31, 1960
Screen Director's Playhouse ("Hot Cargo") January 4, 1956
Alfred Hitchcock Presents ("Alibi Me") November 11, 1956
The Gale Storm Show: Oh! Susana ("The Magician") December 29, 1956
Mr. Adams and Eve January 4, 1957 – September 23, 1958
Studio 57 ("The Alibi") February 6, 1957
Telephone Time ("I Get Along Without You Very Well") November 12, 1957
The Adventures of Jim Bowie ("The Bridegroom") November 29, 1957
The People's Choice ("The Practical Joker") March 20, 1958
The Bob Cummings Show ("Bob Helps Anna Maria") October 7, 1958
The Danny Thomas Show ("Double Dinner") April 20, 1959
The David Niven Show ("A Day of Small Miracles") May 19, 1959
The Donna Reed Show ("Operation Deadbeat") June 3, 1959
Have Gun — Will Travel ("Gold and Brimstone") June 20, 1959
Tightrope ("The Casino") September 15, 1959
Richard Diamond, Private Detective ("The Hoodlum") October 5, 1959
Lincoln-Mercury Startime ("The Jazz Singer") October 13, 1959
The Man from Blackhawk ("Vendetta for the Lovelorn") November 20, 1959
Death Valley Days ("Emma is Coming") May 24, 1960
The Flintstones September 30, 1960 – March 25, 1966
Peter Loves Mary October 12, 1960 – May 31, 1961
Michael Shayne ("The Poison Pen Club") November 25, 1960
Angel ("The Wedding Gift") January 5, 1961
Hennesey ("The Wedding") March 27, 1961
The Gertrude Berg Show ("Dad's Day") March 29, 1962

The New Hanna-Barbera Cartoon Series 1962 – 1963

The Jetsons ("Elroy's Mob") March 17, 1963

The Lucy Show ("Lucy Visits the White House") March 25, 1963

The Jimmy Dean Show (debut show) September 19, 1963

The Dick Van Dyke Show ("The Masterpiece") October 2, 1963

My Favorite Martian ("The Awful Truth") November 17, 1963

Mickey September 16, 1964 – January 13, 1965

The Adventures of Hoppity Hooper ("Ring-a-Ding Spring" and "The Thing in the Spring") September 26, 1964

90 Bristol Court: Harris Against the World ("Harris Against His Secretary") October 5, 1964

The Beverly Hillbillies ("Teenage Idol") November 18, 1964

The Beverly Hillbillies ("The Widow Poke Arrives") November 25, 1964

90 Bristol Court: Harris Against the World ("Harris Against the Studio") November 30, 1964

The Addams Family ("Cousin Itt Visits the Addams Family") February 5, 1965

The Smothers Brothers Show ("Outside Inside Hollywood") January 7, 1966

Dr. Kildare ("A Few Hearts, A Few Flowers") February 7, 1966

Dr. Kildare ("Some Tales for Halloween") February 8, 1966

The Smothers Brothers Show ("We'd Rather Fight Than Switch") February 11, 1966

Honey West ("Pandora's Box") February 11, 1966

Alice in Wonderland, or What's a Nice Kid Like You Doing in a Place Like This March 30, 1966

The Man in the Square Suit ("The Rambling Wreck from Discotheque" April 22, 1966

Space Ghost and Dino Boy ("The Space Ark" and "The Sacrifice" and "Glasstor") December 17, 1966

Batman ("Penguin Sets a Trend") February 1, 1967

Voyage to the Bottom of the Sea ("Destroy Seaview!") March 19, 1967

The Mothers-In-Law ("Through the Lurking Glass") November 26, 1967

The Beverly Hillbillies ("The Great Tag-Team Match") February 7, 1968

Petticoat Junction ("Bad Day at Shady Rest") March 2, 1968

In Name Only November 25, 1969

Where's Huddles? July 1, 1970 – September 9, 1970

Homewood ("The Plot to Overthrow Christmas") December 25, 1970

The Tonight Show with Johnny Carson (Flintstones reunion) November 4, 1971

The Pebbles and Bamm-Bamm Show 1971-76

The Flintstones Comedy Hour September 9, 1972 – January 26, 1974

The Flintstones Comedy Show

STAGE

Broadway
    1940 Love's Old Sweet Song
    1941 Hope for a Harvest
    1942-43 The Pirate

National Tour
    1946 Merry Wives of Windsor

Los Angeles
    (Date Unknown) Twelfth Night
    (Date Unknown) Oasis in Manhattan
    (Date Unknown) Barefoot in the Park
    (Date Unknown) The Impossible Years

As co-founder of Theater Forty in Beverly Hills, appeared in various plays with that organization.

Index

Actors & Sin, 99

Abie's Irish Rose, 68-69, 83

Alan Reed Enterprises, 91, 101, 105

Allen, Fred, 55, 62, 67-68, 73-78, 83, 138-147

"Baby Snooks' daddy," 68

Benaderet, Bea, 110-111

Bergman, Teddy, 13-14, 21, 28, 41, 55, 63, 91, 96

Big Sister, 58

Blanc, Mel, 66, 101, 110-111, 113

"Blubber Bergman," 63-64

Breakfast at Tiffany's, 95, 102

Brown, John, 58, 143

Butler, Daws, 111

Cantor, Charlie, 77, 142, 145, 147

Cantor, Eddie, 55, 62-63, 77

Cisco Kid, 68

Coburn, Charles, 89

"Col. Stoopnagle," 61-63

Conried, Hans, 66-67

Copake Country Club, 48, 51-52, 56

Corden, Henry, 113

Davis, Bette, 47

Days of Glory, 91, 95-96

Double Dummy, 89

Eldridge, Florence, 84, 89

Falstaff's Fables, 78

Far Horizons, The, 100-101

"Flintstone, Fred," 5, 109-111, 113-114, 117-118, 127, 135

Flintstones, The, 6, 66-68, 77, 106, 109-115, 117-119, 125, 127, 135

Fontanne, Lynn, 84, 89

Fred Allen Show, The, 62, 77-78, 83

Garfield, John, 97-98

Gordon, Bert "The Mad Russian," 87

Hart, Moss, 46-47, 51, 56

Harv and Esther, 60

Heller, George, 55, 58

Henry and George, 56, 59-60

Hope, Bob, 87

Hope for a Harvest, 84, 89

House in the Country, A, 89

"Joe Palooka," 64, 69

Kuhn, Walt, 44-45

Life with Luigi, 67, 71-72, 106

Love's Old Sweet Song, 84, 89

Lunt, Alfred, 82, 84, 89

Lux Radio Theatre, 72

Man Called Flintstone, The, 111

March, Frederic, 84, 89

Marjorie Morningstar, 101-102

Merry Wives of Windsor, The, 78-79, 89

Meyer the Buyer, 64

My Friend Irma, 71

Myrt and Marge, 58-59

"Oppenshaw, Falstaff," 5, 62, 67-68, 73-74, 77-79, 146

Peck, Gregory, 85. 91

Peggy Windsor's Letters, 71

Pirate, The, 82-85, 89

Polesi, Herb, 51, 56, 59

Postman Always Rings Twice, The, 11, 95, 97-98

Pyle, Jean Vander, 110-111, 113

Quo Vadis, 84-85

Reed, Finette (Walker), 55, 70, 90-92, 98, 109, 131, 135, 139, 142, 144, 145, 147

Reed, Jr., Alan, 5, 45, 51-52, 70, 90, 92, 96-97, 99, 111, 114, 117, 127, 132-133, 135

"Rubinoff," 62-63

Ryan, Tim & Irene, 105

Schaden, Chuck, 5, 56, 106, 113

Selwyn, Edgar, 12
Seniors, The, 95, 125-127
Shadow, The, 69
Shinbone Alley, 125
Skank, Charlie, 56
That's Rich, 99
Thompson, Bill, 110
Tone, Franchot, 42

Tracy, Spencer, 48
Twelfth Night, 88-89
Vance, Vivian, 91
Viva Zapata!, 96
Welles, Orson, 58
"White Clown, The," 44-45
Wolfe, Jaques, 51

CPSIA information can be obtained at www.ICGtesting.com
Printed in the USA
BVOW030022080312

284675BV00005B/78/P